STYLISH
CAKES

STYLISH CAKES

THE EXTRAORDINARY CONFECTIONS
OF THE FASHION CHEF

CHARLOTTE NEUVILLE

WITH MICHAEL COFFINDAFFER

HARPER DESIGN
An Imprint of HarperCollins Publishers

HarperCollins books may be purchased for educational, business, or sales promotional use. For information please e-mail the Special Markets Department at SPsales@harpercollins.com.

First published in 2015 by
Harper Design
An Imprint of HarperCollins*Publishers*

195 Broadway
New York, NY 10007
Tel: (212) 207-7000
Fax: (855) 746-6023
harperdesign@harpercollins.com
www.hc.com

Distributed throughout the world by
HarperCollins*Publishers*
195 Broadway
New York, NY 10007

ISBN 978-0-06-232812-0

Library of Congress Control Number: 2013950297

Book design by Lynne Yeamans

Printed in China
First Printing, 2015

For my mother, Christiane

CONTENTS

INTRODUCTION

FASHION, A SENSE OF STYLE, AND FINE FOOD all have been an inherent part of my life for as long as I can remember. French was my first language, as my European parents had immigrated to the United States from Paris in 1948, three years before I was born. My father, Jacques, was a dashing and handsome home decor buyer for I. Magnin, the legendary high-fashion and luxury specialty store based in San Francisco. He was also an accomplished painter and draftsman, with a keen eye for color and composition. I was practically raised at I. Magnin: I have very clear memories of strolling along the Chanel-perfumed first-floor aisles, the sound of highly coiffed saleswomen cooing, "There goes Jacques's daughter," wafting behind me.

My father, who began his career at Gump's in 1951, was fond of citing Richard Gump's motto "Good taste costs no more." He moved on to I. Magnin in 1953, when I was one and a half years old. His responsibilities there took him all over the world to purchase one-of-a-kind antiques and objects and to collaborate with artisans to create exclusive designs for the store. His work seemed so exotic, and I saved the many postcards he sent home while on his travels.

My childhood home was a reflection of my father's sophisticated tastes, a life informed by beauty. We had an extensive collection of books in many different languages—German, Italian, French, and English. My parents were both voracious readers, and books, especially art books, held center stage in our living room. One of my earliest pastimes was to sit with my father and thumb through art books on Alberto Giacometti and Leonardo da Vinci. It made me feel very important and grown up that he would share his books with me. These sessions together marked the beginning of my art history education, as my father would discuss the artists and then ask my opinion of their ideas and work.

Although my father spoke English well, my mother, Christiane, arrived in San Francisco speaking only French. She somehow learned to speak English, to cook, and to drive while raising two daughters, often alone, as my father was traveling the world. She came to speak English beautifully, though, and became a highly regarded dean of college counseling for San Francisco University High School. She was smart as a whip—not to mention curious, highly gracious, and, above all, practical. Years later, she would also become my trusted best friend.

Christiane was of firm convictions in all matters culinary. She became a gourmet cook, much to my chagrin as an adolescent. I used to beg for a "normal hamburger" when the *rôti de boeuf* arrived at the dinner table. The kitchen was unquestionably and completely her domain and off-limits to my sister and me. Hence, my "cooking" experience was limited to making elaborate mud pies in our neighbor's garden path. My grandmother, Jeanne, whom we called Goupi, used to save her empty tinfoil pie tins (she loved Swanson frozen pies!) for that express purpose.

The first time my mother allowed me into her kitchen, I was eight years old. We would work side by side, each on our own projects. My first baking specialty was buttermilk pound cake, although I once used the wrong measuring cup and ended up with double the amount of flour in the batter—six cups, instead of three. The batter had to be thrown out, and I was devastated. I never made *that* mistake again. I eventually perfected the cake, and I'm pleased to share the recipe for it with you on page 23.

Far left: My mother and me, 1953. Left: At eight months old, with my parents, 1952. Below left: With Madeleine (right) and my mother, 1963. Below: My mother's Buttermilk Pound Cake recipe card.

BUTTERMILK POUND CAKE
1 cup butter or margarine
2 cups sugar
4 eggs
3 cups sifted all purpose flour
1/2 tsp. soda
1/2 tsp. salt
1 cup buttermilk
1 tsp. vanilla

Cream butter thoroughly until quite fluffy. Now beat sugar in, a little at a time, until mixture is quite light. Beat eggs in, one at a time, very thoroughly. Sift together flour soda, and salt. Mix together buttermilk

Women's World

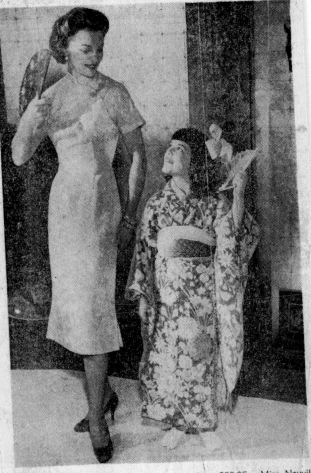

MODEL MARIEL CULVER (left) and little Charlotte Neuville participated in the opening of the Far Eastern Gallery at I. Magnin Monday. Miss Culver is wearing a modern adaptation of an Oriental style in pure silk presentation brocade from the Dynasty collection. It comes in flowering plum, blue, beige and white, priced at $59.95. Miss Neuville's costume is a little girl's ceremonial kimono with scarlet obi and pink sash, one of an extensive collection of Oriental art and fashion to be seen at Magnin's during the two-week Pageant of the Far East, with exhibits on seven floors. A $100,000 cultured pearl exhibit is in the gallery

Left: At age six, in the San Francisco Chronicle, *1958. Right: At seventeen, 1968. Below: In Fire Island, 1978.*

Because I wanted my mother to invite me back to bake with her, I always made sure to leave the kitchen sparkling clean according to her exacting standards. Even though cleaning up thoroughly was part of the experience, I remember thinking the baking thing was worth pursuing and soon became known for my desserts, especially French fruit tarts. My father was my target audience. He loved dessert, and I always strived to make him happy and proud of my accomplishments.

My mother also had an unerring sense of style. For many years, she sewed dresses for my younger sister, Madeleine, and me, although she always bought a new dress for each of us at I. Magnin for the first day of school. Of course, it was a special treat to be taken there to shop. With its pristine white Carrara marble, I. Magnin was the temple of chic. I attended my first fashion show there—that of designer James Galanos—when I was six. At that time, I. Magnin had in-house models and staged private fashion shows so their best customers could preview the new season's garments and place custom orders on the spot. I remember sitting in the front row, gazing in rapture at the models—with their bouffant hairdos and false eyelashes—towering above me as they sauntered down the runway. I felt so special to be there, and the experience cemented my love of fashion at that very moment! I wanted so badly to be a part of that glamorous world, and to this day, I'm sure this early exposure to style was a catalyst for my becoming a fashion designer.

A year after attending my first runway show, I had the opportunity to participate in a different kind of show—and I couldn't have been more thrilled. In April 1958, my father opened the Far Eastern Gallery on I. Magnin's mezzanine, the first in a series of annual events that he launched for the store for many subsequent years. That first year, he recruited me to model as a young Japanese girl. A "geisha" wrapped the traditional obi around my waist and tied my jet-black hair into a tight knot. I was in sheer heaven! A photograph of me with one of the I. Magnin fashion models even appeared in the *San Francisco Chronicle*. After that, I became keen on following fashion (now that I had modeled myself!).

I recall very fondly the first Chanel suit my father brought home from Paris for my mother in the early 1960s. I was in awe of and totally transfixed by the elaborate details, like the delicate silk label and trademark gold chain that was hand-sewn into the nubby wool jacket. At the time, my mother bore a striking resemblance to Jackie Kennedy, complete with bouffant hair that she had set every week at the local hair salon. She was beautiful.

By the time I was in high school, I was still enamored with fashion and treasured my *Seventeen* magazine subscription, especially when Twiggy was featured on the cover. My best friend, Jessie, and I spent hours after school practicing new eye makeup techniques in front of the mirror before we went to our favorite vintage clothing store in San Francisco.

Although I loved fashion, I never thought about it as a career until I finished college, where I studied art history and studio art. I thought I wanted to be a painter, which did not make my parents particularly happy, as they had funded my Ivy League education. Upon returning to California, I grew increasingly disillusioned with the idea of painting as a viable profession. I concluded that I was not willing to run the risk of becoming a starving artist, and I figured if I wasn't willing to starve for my vocation, then I hadn't chosen the appropriate field of study.

One afternoon while eagerly thumbing through my monthly issue of *Vogue*, I had an epiphany: "*This* is what I ought to be doing! I love fashion and style! I should be a fashion designer and ditch the idea of being a painter, once and for all!" Not long after that, I made plans to attend Parsons School of Design in New York City. While still in San Francisco, I wrote to Diana Vreeland, who had become the Metropolitan Museum of Art's special consultant to the Costume Institute the year before, for a job. As luck would have it, she took me on as a volunteer to work in the Costume Institute's restoration department.

Upon arriving in New York in the summer of 1974, I worked on Mrs. Vreeland's first exhibition, *The World of Balenciaga*. I felt like Audrey Hepburn portraying the ebullient side of Holly Golightly in *Breakfast at Tiffany's*: at that point in my life, I didn't think things could get any better. I was in

New York City, where I was meant to be. I was doing what I was meant to: running errands for Mrs. Vreeland and her staff; digging through bins of faux pearls in the Garment District; mending Katharine Hepburn's wedding dress from *The Philadelphia Story*; and combing the Costume Institute's vast archives, from Charles James gowns to Poiret evening robes. To top it off, I was invited to and attended the Met Ball (now known as the Costume Institute Gala). I was dazzled by the experience, having rubbed shoulders with the fashion designer Bob Mackie and Cher, who wore the scandalous and now-famous sheer costume he had created especially for her.

The following summer, after my first year at Parsons, I was asked to work at the Costume Institute again, this time on the *Romantic and Glamorous Hollywood Design* exhibition. Mrs. Vreeland's dynamism was contagious, and it fueled my desire to excel during my three years of study at Parsons so I could land my dream job: to work for Perry Ellis. After graduating in 1977, I worked for Perry Ellis as his design assistant for two years, and then moved on to become Adrienne Vittadini's design director.

In 1985, the same year I married my boyfriend Ken, I decided it was time to start my own business. I registered a sole proprietorship, Charlotte Neuville Studio, to focus on freelance design projects. Soon thereafter, I incorporated my eponymous women's designer sportswear brand, simply named Charlotte Neuville, and was

Above: With my mother, Christiane, 1984.
Right: Charlotte Neuville sportswear in WWD, *1988.*

Left: With Nell, April 1990. Below left: Michael with Nell, 1991.

Left: With Michael, 1991. Above: Jacques and Nell with one of my raspberry tarts, 1995.

inducted into the Council of Fashion Designers of America (CFDA) in 1986. During that time, I had been asked to be a senior critic at Parsons School of Design, and in 1987 I hired one of my favorite students, Michael Coffindaffer. Michael and I became very close friends and collaborators for the duration of my fashion company. Little did I know that we would have the opportunity to reconnect professionally so many years later: he is now my business partner at The Fashion Chef.

In November 1988, I had my first fashion show and landed my first cover on *Women's Wear Daily*. With that, Charlotte Neuville, the brand, was off and running! While designing the fall 1989 collection, I took to wearing Ken's sport jackets to work, and it occurred to me to start designing a version for women. I called the piece "the Boyfriend Jacket"—a description for oversized garments that has now become commonplace in the fashion industry! The year 1990 was monumental, too. First and foremost, my daughter, Nell, was born. Second, my design business was thriving—a dream come true. We received a great deal of media coverage, from *People* and *Vogue* to *Newsweek* and the *New York Times*. The clothes were sold in the finest retailers, including Barneys New York, Neiman Marcus, Lord & Taylor, Bloomingdale's, Saks Fifth Avenue, and Harrods of London.

This period was one of the happiest times of my life. I was designing my own clothes and wearing them every day. I was always experimenting with new proportions, color combinations, and accessories. I was my own guinea pig and walking advertisement, and I thoroughly enjoyed every expressive minute of it!

Far left: Nell and I decorating her sixth birthday cake, 1996. Left: The finished cake. Below: With Nell and Ken, 2000.

I also remember very fondly the great time I had with Michael in the design studio. To blow off steam, we'd spin each other around on the desk chairs, create crazy dress-up combinations, and generally crack each other up with our antics—and I still have a stack of Polaroids to prove it! Our personalities and creative synergy made our design process fluid and an absolute pleasure, even when the pressure was on to raise the bar and outdo last season's collection. Our motto was "Why not?"

I even managed to continue to find time to bake during this period and zeroed in on perfecting French fruit tarts, pecan pie, and President McKinley's Chocolate Cake (a favorite recipe from the 1971 *American Family Cookbook* by Melanie H. De Proft). I also made holiday gift baskets for my buyers, including treats such as homemade quince jam, chocolate dream bars, and my old standby, buttermilk pound cake.

The terrible downside of owning my fashion company was the fact that I was forced to close it—due to lack of funding—in June 1992. The financing plug was pulled with little advance warning, and I felt personally responsible for the welfare of the twenty-six employees who worked for me and had lost their jobs. At that time in the fashion business,

there were few, if any, options to secure alternate investors quickly, so I was left with no other choice than to shutter the business. I won't sugarcoat the truth: having to do that was awful.

Ironically, what kept me sane during this difficult time were the cake-decorating classes I took at the New York Cake and Baking Distribution Company in New York's Chelsea neighborhood. I baked elaborate cakes, practiced my piping technique, and hand-molded and painted marzipan fruit. Nell was my new audience, and with every ensuing year, I conjured ever more complex cakes for her birthday celebrations. When she turned five, I made a "Swiss cheese cake," complete with miniature mice peeking from its holes. Like me, Nell loved to swim, and for her sixth birthday, I made her a cake with three whales spouting "water" in the ocean. During the holidays, I made croquembouches. During the summers, I made my French fruit tarts. All the while, Nell enjoyed being my assistant. I have a photograph of her at one and a half, standing on a chair pouring flour into a mixing bowl—well, just barely. She has since become an accomplished cook and an invaluable assistant at The Fashion Chef when she can spare the time.

In fall 1992, I took a job as senior vice president and creative director for a private-label fashion company. My work there led to a position with Lerner New York in 1996, a division of The Limited. Lerner later become New York & Company, which went private in 2002, and I was named one of the five officers. During this period of my life, I was so consumed with my job that I didn't have the luxury of time to consider baking. Sadly, one of my favorite hobbies was put on hold.

In 2005, I received a call from a recruiter who worked for Gap Inc., asking if I would be interested in running a large segment of corporate design for the company. I couldn't believe my good fortune— I had always dreamed of designing for the Gap. Within two weeks, the news broke in *Women's Wear Daily* that I had joined Gap Inc. as executive vice president of design for menswear, womenswear, and accessories. In this position, I was also responsible for creating the apparel and accessories for the record-breaking global brand PRODUCT (RED) that Bono conceived, raising millions of dollars to combat the AIDS crisis in Africa.

My work on the RED campaign was profound and life-changing. The level of personal self-expression it took to pull off the program, the dedication of a core group of my design team, and the opportunity to potentially affect millions in such a positive way were inspiring

and extraordinary. Plus, I was totally smitten with Bono—what an incredible human being! But my successes at the company were not to last. In February 2007, the executive management team fell apart. One after another, we were asked to leave. I was devastated—yet, oddly enough, thrilled.

For the first time in my adult life, I did not have to work for a while. I had a terrific severance package, and I took advantage of it. I continued to accept interviews, searching for another inspiring position in the fashion industry. Somehow, though, I began to feel like a fish out of water—a bit disconnected. The truth was, at my level in the corporate fashion business, fashion was no longer giving me what I needed.

As an executive vice president of design in a corporate design studio, I was too far removed from being actively creative, and unhappy as a result. In my climb up the corporate ladder, I had become a napkin sketcher—jotting down quick ideas over a business dinner and then handing them off to assistants to develop the next day. While I still adored fashion and considered myself a fashion designer to the core, I was starting to feel like a has-been. The industry was changing dramatically and I found myself questioning how, and even if, I fit into this new landscape.

I started searching elsewhere, first living off my severance and then my savings during this exploratory period of my life, which lasted three years and felt like forever. I wrote and collaged my autobiography and started shopping it around to publish. I got very involved in coaching participants at Landmark Education, which led me to think I should seriously consider becoming a professional coach. I actually went so far as to obtain a certificate in executive and personal coaching from New York University. That idea, however, was short-lived, as I soon discovered that coaching lacked the creative outlets necessary for my well-being. On that much I was clear. So the quandary continued: how to move forward into work that was creative and incorporated my passionate love of fashion.

I struggled with powerful entrepreneurial urges, too. The reality was that the happiest time of my professional life was when I owned my own business, but I knew I didn't want to do it again, at least not in the fashion industry, which had changed so much in the interim. I also worried about the financial risk, particularly as I was now divorced and a single mother.

In 2010, I was invited by a friend to attend a spring dinner party he planned to host. He had seen a cake I had made the week before—and targeted me for dessert duty. I was known among friends and family for my French fruit trifle, and although it's traditionally a Christmas dessert, he requested that I make it for the party. It was a big hit. Those gathered knew of my love of baking and wasted no time pressuring me to consider going professional, or at the very least to check out the French Culinary Institute (now known as the International Culinary Center).

I had visited the school years before on a whim, but now, urged on by my friends, I chose to go for another round. I signed up for a second tour shortly after the party, but once again, I didn't think going back to school was for me. A week later, I received a call from an admissions representative, who mentioned my second visit and offered to answer any questions I might have. He said I was the perfect candidate, exactly what the school was looking for in terms of my background and interests. He persuaded me to come back and take a private tour, during which I had the opportunity to speak with Jacques Pépin and André Soltner, the former chef-owner of the famous French restaurant Lutèce. They were showing off a chocolate showpiece that Jacques Torres (master pastry chef, renowned chocolatier, and another one of the school's deans) had just completed for President Obama, who was in town. We chatted away in French, and I immediately felt right at home. The third time was the charm: within fifteen minutes, I had signed on to take the school's intensive training in the classic French pastry arts. I put my fears aside and took the plunge!

As soon as I had gone to orientation, I walked into career services to request an internship with master cake chef Ron Ben-Israel, the "Manolo Blahnik of wedding cakes." I was politely told that the internship process didn't quite work that way. First, I had to complete my course studies, and then I could submit a résumé and examples of my work for Ron to consider. The advisers there were quick to point out that I had chosen the most competitive internship possible and that if I were lucky enough to get through the initial round of review, I would be asked to set an appointment for a day-long, hands-on interview. Only after this process would I learn if I was accepted to a three-month internship—with no pay.

So with that little reality check, classes began! Being a type A personality, I was determined to excel in school, basically competing against my own standards of perfection. Even though I was now attending school as a fifty-nine-year-old former fashion executive, my approach to academia remained unchanged. I kept my age to myself, as I didn't want to be coddled or judged differently from the twenty-somethings who populated my class.

The Cloud Cake

I soon discovered that it was not as easy for me as it once had been to memorize and retain information; plus, I was a madwoman about perfecting my skills. Case in point: the week we were studying génoise cake, I made no fewer than fifteen of them at home, until I knew for certain that I had it down! And so went the learning curve at the French Culinary Institute. We studied everything my French heritage had ever dreamed of concocting—tarts, *pâte à choux*, puff pastry, crème anglaise, assorted breads and *viennoiseries*, petits fours, chocolate making, and of course all things cake!

I graduated in January 2011 and did land the coveted internship with my idol, Ron Ben-Israel, after all. I stayed for the full three months, learning and absorbing as much as possible about this new business. While I worked for Ron, I got my first two wedding cake orders. I would go home at night and toil on the decorations for hours on end. I even recruited Nell to assist me in making dozens of sugar paste flowers intended for a multi-tier vanilla wedding cake covered in ice blue fondant. I dubbed my creation the Cloud Cake.

The Cloud Cake was a milestone for me. The topper was decorated with white silk chiffon garden roses, and each tier was trimmed with dark chocolate brown double-faced satin ribbon. From the beginning, I have looked for special ways to make a cake unique. For the Cloud Cake, the bride explained that her mother had passed away ten years earlier, and she hoped I might be able to think of a way to commemorate her on the cake with a ladybug, one of her mother's favorite creatures. With that, I found a cherry-red-and-gold enameled ladybug charm that I tucked beneath the roses on the top tier. Unless a guest looked very closely, only the bride and groom knew it was there. Much more than a decoration, that single ladybug became a small but significant memento to the wedding couple.

Despite my positive experience at the French Culinary Institute and a promising start in the pastry arts, I was still terrified of permanently switching career paths at this point in my life, and especially of "losing" fashion after thirty successful years in design. I needed a break and a quiet space alone to think things through. In summer 2011, I packed up my twenty-year-old cat, Mimi, and rented a simple 1920s bungalow in East Hampton on Long Island. Overlooking Three Mile Harbor, the house was a twenty-minute drive to my mother's home in Sag Harbor, which made it all the more compelling. She had relocated from San Francisco after my father's death years before.

I had two main criteria to consider. First, I wanted to live by the water. My bungalow was located on a wooded lot perched on the edge of the harbor. The second-story bedroom allowed extra space to set up a working studio, and both the bedroom and living room overlooked the water. Every morning a bevy of swans would sashay up to the side of the dock, and each evening I enjoyed an exquisite sunset. The location was perfect. My second, and more important, reason for choosing East Hampton was to see whether I wanted to launch a retail

business there. I had imagined a stylish patisserie that sold beautiful items alongside my cakes— handmade papers and stationery, French ribbons, even fresh flowers—all things that I had always loved and appreciated. After weeks of research, interviews, and legwork, I decided not to pursue that course of action. The risks were just too high for such a short selling season, not to mention the exorbitant commercial rental costs. Too many local business owners warned me of the downsides, and when early September rolled around, I packed up Mimi again and headed back to New York. This time, I was very clear and knew what I wanted to do . . . with certainty!

Enter The Fashion Chef.

I had conjured up the name for my business a year or so previously, but in my original concept, The Fashion Chef was a television show. The idea was to invite my fashion designer friends to appear on the program. We would laugh and chat, talk fashion and food trends, and then bake together. The concept was still primarily fashion-focused, so I parked the name in my brain for future consideration.

After my summer in the Hamptons I went full steam ahead with The Fashion Chef, but in a different form than I had originally intended. What I wanted to do more than anything was to create unique cake designs for all celebrations. I imagined reaching out to my connections in the fashion industry to get started—it would be a couture cake business! I believed I was on to something and trademarked The Fashion Chef brand in November 2011.

Just as I had treasured special trimmings in my fashion career, I started collecting and using them in my cake designs—sumptuous silk flowers, ribbons, vintage braids, plumes, feathers, and jewels. In fashion, I had been regarded as a color expert, and I knew that knowledge would help me again. A cake was just a new canvas!

That fall, I officially started my business. I set up shop in my apartment—on my dining-room table. Soon the dining room wasn't big enough, so I transformed my bedroom into the design studio. I bought a second refrigerator, moved it into my ex-bedroom, and continued to bake all my orders out of my home kitchen. My close friends and acquaintances were the first to place orders, and with that initial exposure, one cake quickly led to another. Within a few months, I had to hire my first assistant. I slept on a mattress in the living room. I didn't care—I loved my cake design studio, even if I didn't have a bedroom any longer!

By March 2012, I had launched The Fashion Chef Web site and then reached out to my connections in the fashion industry and my network of associates. I sent an e-mail to practically everyone on my contact list announcing my new business—and honestly, it was all rather intimidating. While at Gap Inc., I had become absorbed in the corporate design world, and my close involvement with the fashion industry and the CFDA had lapsed somewhat. I wondered if my former fashion peers would even be interested in what I was doing five years later, and outside the industry to boot. My fears were quickly put to rest as many people responded enthusiastically to the news, including Ed Filipowski, a treasured acquaintance and copresident with Julie Mannion of KCD, the leading global fashion public relations and production company.

Within days, news got out, and Mark Lee, CEO of Barneys New York, ordered a cake for a private party celebrating Alber Elbaz's ten-year anniversary as Lanvin's creative director. The event was created by one of my favorite caterers, Hank Tomashevski. Hank proved to be an ardent supporter and, as Anna Wintour's personal chef, he had great connections, which provided a number of highly creative cake orders, both for Anna and for an assortment of his other celebrity clients. I felt as if I had come full circle: in the early years of my fashion company, Anna had been incredibly supportive of my work, often featuring me in the pages of American *Vogue*. Mark also put me in contact with the Barneys home decor and gourmet buying team to discuss the possibility of my creating special cakes for the upcoming holiday season. One open door opened many more; I truly felt honored and appreciated—and grateful.

Five months later, in August 2012, my mother, Christiane, passed away after fighting a one-month battle in an intensive care unit. Her death was completely unexpected and left Nell and me devastated. I lost my rock and my best friend. She was an extraordinary human being—outspoken, uncompromising, loyal to a fault, and always supportive of my sister and me, Nell, and her circle of friends. I knew she was concerned that I didn't have a fashion job as the months and years passed, but she held fast to her incredible faith in me, which in turn gave me the courage to keep going. She knew and trusted that I just needed time to experiment and figure out what was next.

And that's why only a week after her death, I attended a meeting with the buying team at Barneys New York to talk about holiday 2012. I remember telling myself, "Christiane would want you to be there, Charlotte—go!" The meeting went very well and we all left enthusiastic about collaborating on exclusive holiday cakes for the store. Knowing I would soon outgrow my design studio at home, I made plans to move my still-young business to a commercial kitchen space by October, one that I would share with Hank as well as the catering team, Martin + Fitch. I had to get myself properly prepared for the Barneys holiday cake orders!

My collaboration with Barneys was successful and grew with the ensuing Valentine's Day and Easter holidays. Talent scouts started to call. In spring 2013, Oprah Winfrey's editorial department at *O, The Oprah Magazine*, contacted me, having seen The Fashion Chef's Easter cakes at Barneys. The Oprah team was planning a major food issue for August, and the editor wanted to know if I would be interested in submitting three cakes for their consideration. I remember thinking to myself, "Interested? You have got to be kidding." I was beyond excited at the opportunity!

There was one daunting caveat, though: if the magazine chose my designs, the three cakes would have to be available for mail order to Oprah's readership via The Fashion Chef's newly minted Web site. I would be required to drop-ship the cakes anywhere in the United States, directly to the customer.

Barely containing my panic, I thought: "Michael!" I knew I couldn't handle this alone, and there was no way I was going to disappoint Oprah and her readers. Michael, my erstwhile design-partner in crime at Charlotte Neuville Inc., had remained in New York and built a successful career as an executive in the home decor and gift industry. He agreed to take on the mail order development for the Oprah project and all that it would entail. I couldn't imagine handling that enormous task without him. He established all the necessary components to ship the cakes perfectly and in time for the magazine's August issue. Then, beyond my wildest dreams, the Oprah team chose

The Fashion Chef's three cakes to appear as the opening page of "The O List"!

Soon thereafter, Michael and I were once again inseparable. After years of friendship, we rediscovered how much we loved working together. After going our separate creative ways, we soon saw how much stronger and complementary our skills had become as a result. By the end of 2013, Michael had signed on with The Fashion Chef as my business partner. We have a renewed synergy, and even though we are so familiar with each other, the element of surprise still exists. There is never a dull moment.

Although it took me a long time to move into the pastry arts, dreaming up The Fashion Chef may just be my best creation yet. The fear of losing fashion in my life was put to rest when I realized I could simply merge my two passions. My connection to fashion is as great as ever as I create special cakes and cake collections for retailers, designers, and editors in the industry as well as for other notable figures.

Most important, I feel creative again, sketching my wildest cake dreams—not on napkins—and interacting with my incredible clients. I'm always on to the next idea and loving every minute of it. As I designed more and more cakes, I noticed that my ideas started to fall into general patterns and themes around many things I have always loved: gardens, bright graphic colors, gold, jewel trims, and, most of all, fashion, beauty, and a great sense of humor!

To say the least, it was an incredible honor to be approached by Elizabeth Viscott Sullivan at HarperCollins, who asked if I would be interested in doing a book of The Fashion Chef's cake creations. After jumping up and down with joy, and then figuring out how to tackle this enormous project, Michael and I were inspired to organize the cakes featured in the book around personal themes. We believe that the best work comes from staying true to what speaks to you personally and following your passion, regardless of the particular medium you are working in.

The book is about taking risks, too. Or at least that's what we hope you take away from reading my story and how I came to create The Fashion Chef: it's never too late to start on a project or career path that's close to your heart.

Before we begin, though, I want to thank my team at The Fashion Chef. I am fortunate to be living my entrepreneurial dreams for the second time in my life, but I could not have achieved them alone. I have wonderfully talented artisans who assist in bringing The Fashion Chef cake creations to life. We all love what we do, laughing and learning as we go, each person contributing in important ways to our mutual success. Together we create The Fashion Chef's one-of-a-kind couture cakes and chic confections, with the goal that each one be as visually unforgettable as it is delicious.

I'm excited and honored to share our work in the following pages. I hope you are wildly inspired by our cakes and confections and will try some of the ideas, recipes, and tutorials found at the end of each chapter. I have always thought of the photographs in this book as "cake art"—and hope you will refer to them time and again when dreaming up your own stylish creations.

—CHARLOTTE NEUVILLE
New York City

Buttermilk Pound Cake

This will make two loaves, 8 × 4 inches, or four loaves, 7 × 3 inches.

This is the recipe I used as a child to make my first specialty! I present it here, exactly as printed on my mother's recipe card.

INGREDIENTS

1 cup butter or margarine

2 cups sugar

4 eggs

3 cups sifted all-purpose flour

½ tsp. baking soda

½ tsp. salt

1 cup buttermilk

1 tsp. vanilla

Cream butter thoroughly until quite fluffy.

Now beat sugar in, a little at a time, until mixture is quite light.

Beat eggs in, one at a time, very thoroughly.

Sift together flour, soda, and salt.

Mix together buttermilk and vanilla.

Add these ingredients alternately to sugar and egg mixture, beginning and ending with dry ingredients and beating thoroughly.

Bake about one hour in a 325° F oven.

This cake is excellent and moist. It slices very thin and can be kept wrapped in foil for a week. It also freezes well.

I.
HOW FRENCH

A walk about Paris will provide lessons in
history, beauty, and in the point of Life.

—Thomas Jefferson

MY FRENCH HERITAGE provided the foundation for my love of the pastry classics. That, along with my fashion background, always inspires me to strive for beauty in my creative endeavors. When I muse on all things aesthetic and classically French, I think of Limoges china: chic, pristine, delicate, and in the softest of pale colors. The combination of these elements is what the cakes in this chapter are really about.

Take the Porcelain Wedding Cake (page 32), for example. My inspiration for it emerged when I met with the clients to review the flowers they had selected for the tablescapes at their wedding reception. What struck me most were the subtle shades of white; I loved that exquisite, sophisticated attention to detail and wanted to capture it on the cake. The Paillette Cake (page 46) is a study in color variations, with shades ranging from soft pinks to creamy peaches to white. Some cakes in this chapter are elaborate, while others are quite simple, like a classic pearl necklace, or the Little Black Dress Cakelettes (page 29) paired with a single understated "pearl," but they all embody a certain refinement and restraint that, to me, is unquestionably French.

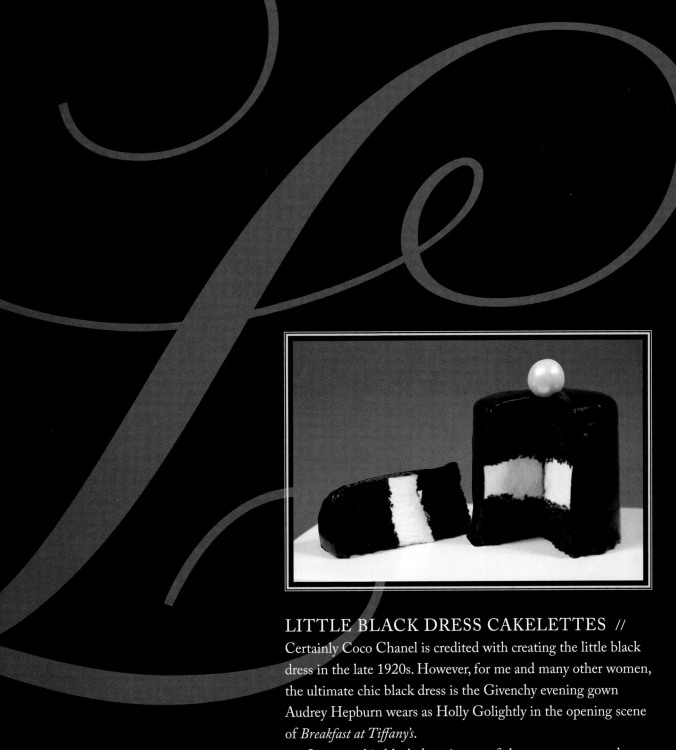

LITTLE BLACK DRESS CAKELETTES //

Certainly Coco Chanel is credited with creating the little black dress in the late 1920s. However, for me and many other women, the ultimate chic black dress is the Givenchy evening gown Audrey Hepburn wears as Holly Golightly in the opening scene of *Breakfast at Tiffany's*.

Just as a chic black dress is part of almost every woman's wardrobe, The Fashion Chef has its own version, our Luxe French Chocolate Cake (recipe on page 50)—a delicately moist chocolate glazed cake—trimmed with a luminous, hand-molded "pearl" crafted in fine white chocolate.

PORCELAIN WEDDING CAKE // Occasionally I have the opportunity to design and create a truly beautiful cake that surpasses all expectations—even my own! That's exactly what happened with this wedding cake, which looks just like exquisite French porcelain.

The cake required dozens and dozens of highly intricate and delicate sugar paste flowers, all rendered in the subtlest shades of white and ivory. The design team created literally hundreds of flowers—lilies-of-the-valley (a personal favorite that always reminds me of my French mother), tiny cherry blossoms reinvented in chalk white, and ruffly ribbonlike flowers, buds, and tea roses—all created in variations of white to delicately surround the bride and groom's monogram.

The client requested that we keep the fondant and decorations matte, which enhanced the porcelain effect.

The bride chose our Luxe French Chocolate Cake (recipe on page 50) in combination with one of my favorite fillings—a maple buttercream that we make with Crown Maple's inimitable organic maple sugar and syrup.

Baby ranunculus stand by, waiting for the big day and final assembly on the cake.

VERSION 2.

FINAL
SKETCH ✳
5" = Flowers

HEIGHT

4½"   4½"

8"   7½"

3"   3¾"

6"   5⅞"

4"   4¼

Final
Measurements
(28" Final)

Faux

DIAMETER

6"

9"

12"

15"

19"

Faux

11¼"

*One highlight of the cake was the monogram, created by the couple's
interwoven initials. The motif was featured throughout the wedding celebration,
from the save-the-date reminders to the wedding cake itself.*

FRENCH PEONY CAKE // While square cakes, with their right angles and crisp edges, present different types of design challenges, they provide a clean canvas from which a design can clearly emerge. For this cake, I chose a version of the client's favorite French blue and accented it with soft white and glittering silver trim. The asymmetric placement of peonies and white parrot tulips softens the cake's geometry. The oversize sparkling curlicues give the cake whimsy and holiday flair.

The mirror base adds another festive touch, reflecting light and highlighting the shapes of the decorations to magical effect.

peonies &
garden roses

Nature, particularly gardens, is a constant source of inspiration for me, as I grew up in Sausalito around my mother's carefully tended flower and foliage garden. Having a garden of my own is still essential to my happiness.

I take great pride in our artistic and technical abilities in re-creating nature with sugar paste flowers, including all manner of roses, lilies of the valley, tiger orchids, lisianthus, and Japanese anemones, among many others. I look for opportunities to incorporate a range of flowers into my cake designs whenever possible.

At left is a single large open peony in delicate sugar paste.

*An exquisite watercolor created by artist Anne Watkins
specifically for the party.*

Height

Diameter

3½"

6"

4½"

9"

5"

12"

5½"

15"

6"

Sugar Paste Flowers with Miniature Lights

White Paillettes are glittered white

Edible Metallic silver band

EMMA

Luxe French Chocolate Cake

Makes two 8-inch cakes

Of the dozens of chocolate cakes I have tasted, Ina Garten's recipe for Beatty's Chocolate Cake is my favorite. I have adapted the recipe slightly, adjusting the number and size of the eggs and using Valrhona cocoa powder specifically. I especially love this cake combined with my Tahitian Vanilla Bean Buttercream (recipe on page 80), which is what we most typically pair with The Fashion Chef's chocolate cakes. A wonderful alternative to the buttercream filling and frosting is my recipe for Chocolate Ganache, which follows.

INGREDIENTS

Unsalted butter, to grease pans

224 grams (1¾ cups) all-purpose flour, plus extra for dusting the cake pans

400 grams (2 cups) granulated sugar

100 grams (¾ cup) Valrhona or other high-quality cocoa powder

2 teaspoons baking soda

1 teaspoon baking powder

1 teaspoon kosher salt

240 milliliters (1 cup) buttermilk, shaken

120 milliliters (½ cup) vegetable oil

3 large eggs, at room temperature

1 teaspoon pure vanilla extract

240 milliliters (1 cup) freshly brewed hot coffee

Preheat the oven to 350° F.

Grease two 8 × 2–inch round cake pans with unsalted butter. Line them with parchment paper, butter them again, and dust lightly with flour.

Sift the flour, sugar, cocoa powder, baking soda, baking powder, and salt into the bowl of a standing electric mixer fitted with the paddle attachment. Mix on low speed until incorporated.

In a medium mixing bowl, blend the buttermilk, oil, eggs, and vanilla. With the mixer on low speed, slowly add the wet ingredients to the dry ingredients. Add the coffee, taking care to not overmix. Scrape the sides and bottom of the bowl with a rubber spatula.

Pour the batter into the prepared pans. Bake for 35 to 40 minutes, until a cake tester comes out clean. Cool the cakes in the pans for 30 minutes, then turn them out onto a wire rack to cool completely.

Chocolate Ganache

Covers and fills a two-layer 8-inch cake

Chocolate ganache is an alternative to covering a cake in buttercream and fondant. Ganache is quick and easy to make and acts as a protective coating to seal in the cake's moisture.

INGREDIENTS

615 grams (2½ cups) fine semisweet or bittersweet chocolate, finely chopped

235 milliliters (1 cup) heavy cream

Place the chocolate in a medium stainless-steel bowl. Heat the heavy cream in a medium heavy-bottomed saucepan until it just begins to simmer. Make certain that the cream does not boil over.

Pour the cream into the center of the bowl of chocolate and let it stand for 1 or 2 minutes. Then stir the chocolate/cream mixture with a rubber spatula until completely smooth. Scrape down the sides of the bowl with the spatula.

Allow the ganache to come to room temperature in the bowl. Stir it occasionally, making certain that the chocolate has completely melted. Once the ganache has cooled down, pour it into a plastic microwave-safe lidded container and refrigerate it for 1 hour. This allows the ganache to set and crystallize, creating the desired consistency.

Remove the ganache from the refrigerator. Microwave it in 10-second intervals, scraping and stirring the mixture each time until it reaches room temperature. You may have to do this in several batches, depending on how much ganache you need.

Ganache can be refrigerated for up to 5 days or kept frozen up to 1 month. Frozen ganache must be thawed before it can be reconstituted to the correct consistency. Once the ganache thaws to room temperature, beat it with a wooden spoon until smooth.

II.
A SHOT OF COLOR

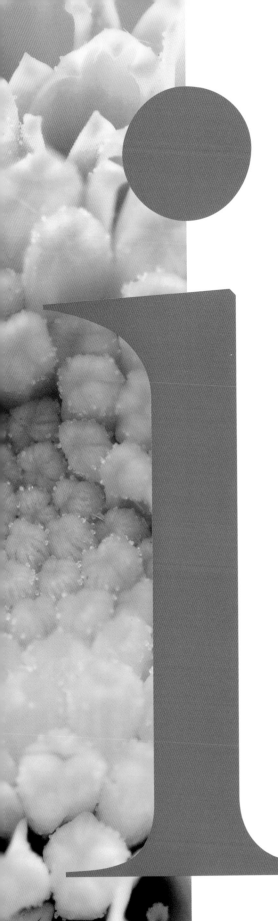

I AM CRAZY IN LOVE WITH COLOR! It is truly one of my greatest passions.

When I was a fashion designer, color was unfailingly the springboard of every collection. More often than not, the fabric colors and patterns provided major inspiration for the design of the clothes themselves. My color inspiration came from countless sources: a lushly winter-colored Italian plaid, a frosty stripe combination from a French silk mill, or an exuberantly painted print of hot pink peonies. The color choices were always a critical component of the design process.

In this chapter, there are many examples of how closely colors and fabrics relate to the cakes you see here. A classic red-and-white-checked tablecloth provided the perfect oversize graphic for the Summer Barbecue Cake (page 56), while the Ribbon Cake (page 77) is an homage to an exquisite two-tone iridescent silk stripe that I used in one of my evening sportswear collections years ago. The green-and-pink color combination for the Graphic Monogram "N" Cake (page 62) practically vibrates with preppy color excitement.

Choosing a fondant color is one thing, but mixing it is another, and it is often a tricky business. Some colors are really lovely to look at and might be the perfect choice for an evening dress, but I am always mindful that our fondant and sugar paste colors must be breathtakingly beautiful and appetizing. I stay away from muddy colors, preferring a stronger, clearer palette. The Fashion Chef cakes possess visual punch: I love bright, saturated colors, especially when used in unusual combinations to create cakes that are fresh, crisp, vibrant, and, most of all, happy.

PHOTOGRAPHS BY GREGOR HALENDA

miniature cake trio

When the editors at *O, The Oprah Magazine* selected The Fashion Chef to create exclusive cake designs for Oprah's "O List" in a summer food issue, they expressed a real interest in the novelty of our four-inch miniature cakes. I was thrilled—and my mind immediately started to race with new ideas for our petite round canvases. Here are the three designs that ultimately found their way into the magazine.

SUMMER BARBECUE CAKE // One of my favorite summer pastimes was to hang out with friends, enjoying their company in the glorious warm weather. This cake (opposite)—complete with a checkered tablecloth and set with a plate of iconic picnic treats—reminds me of quintessential summertime pleasures. I'm especially fond of its tiny scale and the amount of detail we lavished on these petite sugar paste decorations. The cake itself is four inches in diameter, the plate just two inches across, the corn on the cob and hot dog no more than one and a half inches in length, and the wee pickle a mere seven-eighths of an inch long. The hot dog has a squirt of mustard, the corn is buttered, and the pickle looks like it just came out of the jar. All in all, this cake has proved to be a real crowd-pleaser in miniature.

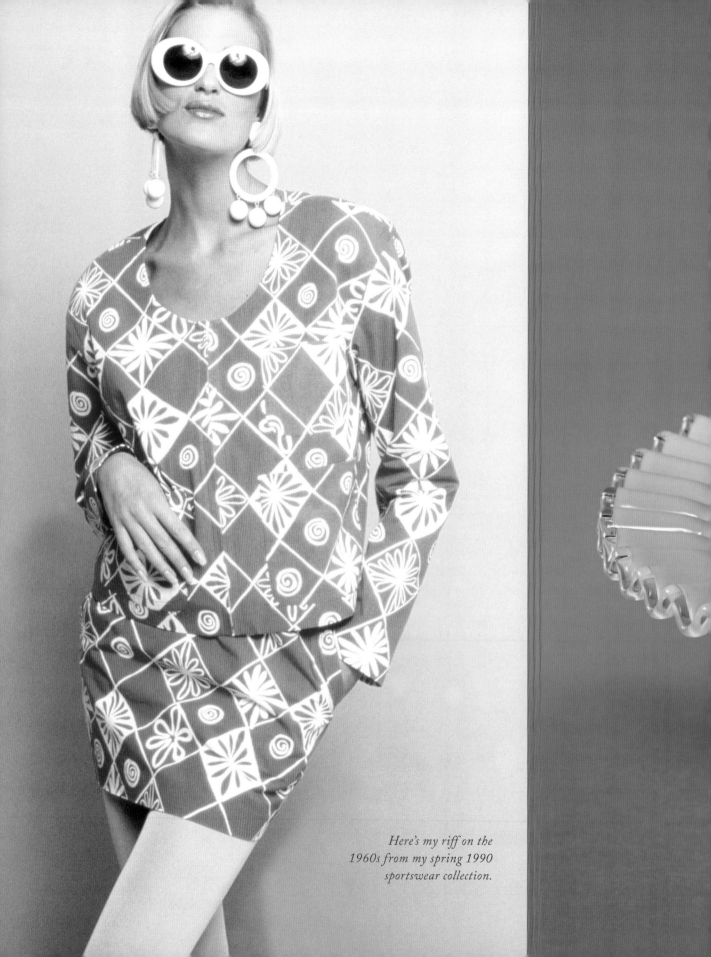

*Here's my riff on the
1960s from my spring 1990
sportswear collection.*

EVERYTHING'S COMING UP DAISIES // I love the color orange and am a huge fan of daisies, so this cake was not only a treat to design, but it also feels like a little ray of sunshine. The daisy is made from a food-safe silicone mold—a must-have when you have so many of one form to duplicate. With a sunny yellow center and little white sculpted petals, each daisy is just seven-eighths of an inch in diameter.

This design is popular in larger sizes, too, as seen in the six-inch cake pictured here.

BEE HAPPY CAKE //

Without a doubt, the most charming aspect of this cake is the tiny, smiling, buzzing bees that have landed on the Swiss dot ribbons. The Bee Happy Cake has proved to be quite popular for a variety of celebrations, always a pick-me-up for a friend in need of welcome cheer. Measuring a diminutive half inch, each bee is completely handcrafted, down to its three stripes and happy little face.

In this photograph, each bee has been left to dry on the end of a wooden toothpick.

graphic monogram cakes

I'm often asked to incorporate a client's name or initials onto a cake, so I'm always challenging myself to come up with fresh and exciting ways to reinterpret them into the overall design theme.

These monogram cakes provide eye-popping solutions with their bold and graphic statements, in which the monogram, color choices, and cake pattern are all considered equally in the overall design concept. Endlessly combining and mixing the patterned elements and monogram styles provides an opportunity for me to create cakes unique to the personality of the lucky recipient.

PSYCHEDELIC CAKE // Growing up in San Francisco, I collected many of the Fillmore's posters, which creatively headlined its music gigs through the use of bold graphic design and psychedelic color. When creating a cake to celebrate a client's milestone birthday, we were asked to reference 1960s pop culture, so we had plenty of inspiration to draw from. Using one of my vintage posters as our primary reference, as well as a photograph of our client as a young man, we hand-painted his image onto the cake, transforming his long hair into stylized peacock feathers that wrap around the cake. We also created our own hippie-inspired font that announced his birthday as if he were the next big act at the Fillmore. Peace, man.

your name in lights

I was first inspired to incorporate LED lights onto a cake when Mark Lee, the CEO of Barneys New York, asked me to create a Disney-themed cake for a private party honoring Bob Iger, the chairman and chief executive officer of the Walt Disney Company. The party was a celebration of the Disney-Barneys collaboration that had culminated in Electric Holiday, the Barneys New York holiday presentation, for which I had created a group of Disney-inspired cakes. I designed a three-tier cake, with a top tier that sported sugar paste Mickey Mouse ears. Decorated entirely with miniature multicolored LED lights, the cake was a twinkling, festive display of color.

I knew I was onto something with those LED lights! I particularly enjoyed using them for the Paillette Cake (see page 46) and for the other bat mitzvah cakes featured in this chapter.

"Samantha and Rachel" was piped in block letters on tiny sugar paste "bubbles" that floated in a sea of pearlized gelatin bubbles, sugar paste glitter balls, and miniature LED lights. These were attached to the brightly hued cake that coordinated with the event's color scheme.

RIBBON CAKE // When I was a fashion designer, one of the most memorable fabrics I ever used for my evening sportswear collections came from Lyons, France— a dreamy two-tone iridescent stripe silk in three luscious colorways: lime green, lemon yellow, and a beautiful sherbet orange. I loved this stripe so much, I designed a whole collection around it and even had Manolo Blahnik create coordinating mules from the same fabric. Aside from its amazing colors, the fabric had the most beautiful ribbonlike sheen that still feels as fresh to me today as it did then.

I wanted to re-create the fabric in cake form, and my assistant Ely jumped at the opportunity to interpret the fabric in sugar paste. I was able to create that pearlized sheen I loved so much, and I decided that it was just enough on its own—so I kept each tier simple and modern. The complete recipe for this cake is on page 80.

Opposite: A look from my Charlotte Neuville sportswear collection featuring the fabric that inspired the Ribbon Cake.

The cake itself is The Fashion Chef's classic Tahitian Vanilla Bean Butter Cake (recipe on page 80). I chose three different buttercream flavors to coordinate with the cake's colors: key lime filling for lime green, lemon filling for lemon yellow, and a passion fruit filling to represent sherbet orange.

Tahitian Vanilla Bean Butter Cake

Makes two 9-inch cakes

This is our standard recipe for all The Fashion Chef's vanilla cakes. I love this recipe because the cake has a dense texture and not too sweet a flavor that provides a perfect foil for a wide range of buttercreams. The cake's firm body allows it to support a lot of sugar paste decorations—obviously important in our line of work!

INGREDIENTS

340 grams (3 sticks) unsalted butter, at room temperature, plus extra for greasing the cake pans

400 grams (2 cups) granulated sugar

6 large eggs, at room temperature

1 tablespoon pure vanilla extract, preferably Tahitian

385 grams (3 cups) all-purpose flour, plus extra for dusting the cake pans

1 teaspoon baking powder

½ teaspoon baking soda

½ teaspoon kosher salt

240 milliliters (1 cup) buttermilk, shaken

Preheat the oven to 350° F.

Butter two 9 × 2–inch cake pans. Line with parchment paper, then butter them again and dust lightly with flour.

In the bowl of a standing electric mixer fitted with the paddle attachment, cream the butter and sugar together on medium-high speed for 3 to 5 minutes, until the mixture is light and fluffy.

Lower the mixer speed to medium. Add the eggs, one by one, into the bowl, scraping down the bowl with a rubber spatula during the process. Add the vanilla and mix until incorporated.

Sift together the flour, baking powder, baking soda, and kosher salt into a medium mixing bowl.

With the mixer on low speed, alternate the dry ingredients with the buttermilk, beginning and ending with the dry ingredients. Do not overmix.

Pour the batter into the prepared pans. Bake in the center of the oven for 45 to 50 minutes, until the tops are browned and a cake tester comes out clean. Cool on a large wire baking rack for 30 minutes, then turn the cakes out onto the rack to finish the cooling process.

Tahitian Vanilla Bean Buttercream

Makes 6 cups, enough to fill and crumb-coat one 9-inch round cake, assuming that one layer of buttercream is ¼ inch thick and that you are using 3 layers of cake

This recipe gets a big workout at The Fashion Chef, as it is often our starting point for creating an infinite variety of buttercream flavors.

INGREDIENTS

300 grams (1½ cups) granulated sugar

215 milliliters (1 cup) or 5½ egg whites or pasteurized egg whites in liquid form

545 grams (2¼ cups or 4¾ sticks) unsalted butter, cubed and softened

Pinch of salt

5 milliliters (1 teaspoon) pure Tahitian vanilla extract

½ teaspoon Tahitian vanilla bean paste

In the bowl of a standing electric mixer fitted with the whip attachment, whisk the sugar and the egg whites together on low speed until just combined.

Bring a pot of water to the boil. Set a stainless-steel mixing bowl over the pot, making certain that the base of the bowl does not touch the boiling water.

Heat the sugar–egg whites mixture until the sugar is dissolved and the mixture is hot. The temperature should register 140 to 150° F on a candy thermometer (or on a Thermapen, which is my favorite instant-read thermometer. See Select Sources, page 237). Whisk the mixture constantly.

Put the bowl back in the mixer, beating on high speed until the mixture forms a stiff meringue. This procedure will take approximately 10 minutes. The meringue should be at room temperature.

At this point, stop the mixer, remove the whip, and install the paddle attachment. At low speed, gradually add the butter and salt to the meringue. Once all the butter has been blended, the mixer can be turned to medium speed. Beat until fluffy.

Add the vanilla extract and the paste. Once the vanilla is blended, scrape the bowl with a rubber spatula and continue to mix on medium speed until the mixture has achieved a smooth and creamy consistency.

If you do not use the buttercream immediately, you can store it in an airtight container at room temperature for up to 6 hours. Refrigerated, it will keep for 1 week; frozen, for 6 months.

If the buttercream has been refrigerated or frozen, it must be brought to room temperature before using. Place it in the bowl of the mixer with the paddle attachment, and beat until it has been restored to its smooth consistency. Do not be concerned if it appears curdled during the beating process.

Buttercream Variations

Here are the three variations on the Tahitian Vanilla Bean Buttercream recipe that we used to create the three fillings for the Ribbon Cake.

Prepare the Tahitian Vanilla Bean Buttercream recipe and divide it into thirds. This will allow for 2 cups of each buttercream for each cake. Add and combine the ingredients below to each third.

If you wish to tint the buttercream, do so very carefully by adding one drop of gel-paste coloring at a time until you achieve the color you desire. Do not add too much coloring; if you do, the buttercream will become runny.

KEY LIME BUTTERCREAM

2 cups (454 grams) buttercream

1½ tablespoons Amoretti Artisan Natural Flavor: Key Lime

⅛ teaspoon powdered citric acid

LEMON BUTTERCREAM

2 cups (454 grams) buttercream

½ tablespoon fresh Amoretti Lemon Compound #304

⅛ teaspoon powdered citric acid

PASSION FRUIT BUTTERCREAM

2 cups (454 grams) buttercream

½ tablespoon Amoretti Artisan Natural Flavor: Passion Fruit

⅛ teaspoon powdered citric acid

III.
NIGHT AND DAY

The opulence of the Metropolitan Club setting enhanced
the fairy tale–like quality of this special event.

MINIATURE CELEBRATION BUBBLE CAKES //

The Fashion Chef's four-inch-diameter miniature cake is a favorite of ours and our clients—it's quite popular for intimate dinners for two. We design this cake in a range of colors and flavors year-round and for all sorts of celebrations. When decorated with our signature bubbles and glitter balls, this petite cake becomes a party unto itself.

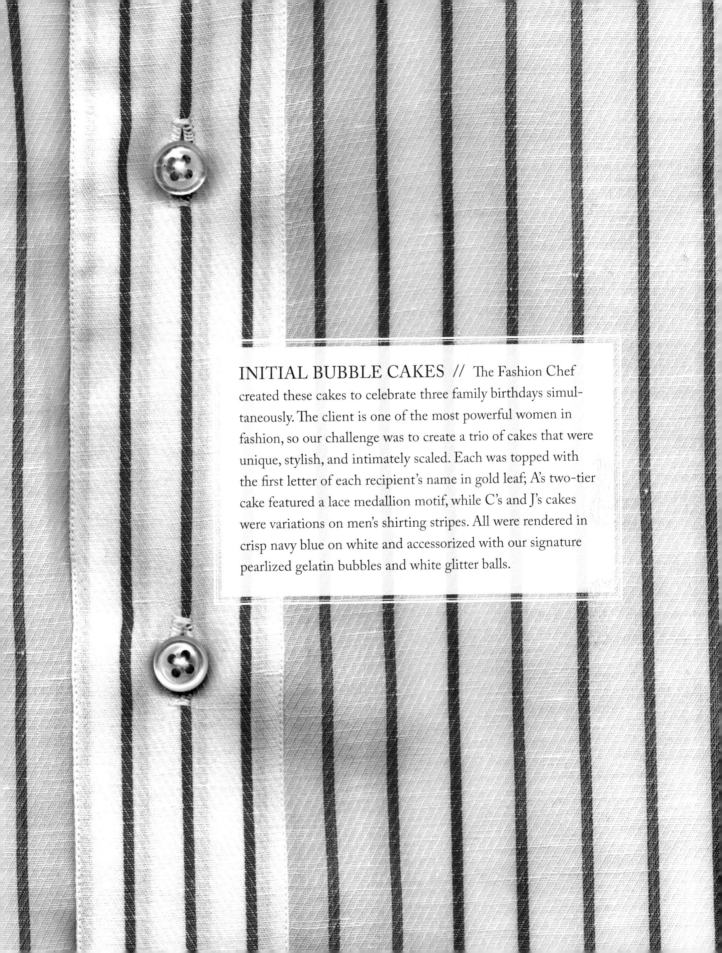

INITIAL BUBBLE CAKES // The Fashion Chef created these cakes to celebrate three family birthdays simultaneously. The client is one of the most powerful women in fashion, so our challenge was to create a trio of cakes that were unique, stylish, and intimately scaled. Each was topped with the first letter of each recipient's name in gold leaf; A's two-tier cake featured a lace medallion motif, while C's and J's cakes were variations on men's shirting stripes. All were rendered in crisp navy blue on white and accessorized with our signature pearlized gelatin bubbles and white glitter balls.

"SPLAT!" COOKIE // The ubiquitous black-and-white cookie is universally loved but definitely due for a fashion makeover, inside and out! Here we introduce jazzed-up, thoroughly modern "Splat!" Cookies, inspired by the work of abstract expressionist Jackson Pollock. I'm a big fan of this particular *Galettes Sablées* ("Sugar Cookies") recipe and share it with you on page 114.

S

"SPLAT!" CAKE // We had so much fun decorating our "Splat!" Cookies, we decided to up the ante on this two-tier confection, previously a proper and demure cake topped with pristine sugar paste flowers. The juxtaposition of these seemingly disparate concepts is completely modern. Plus you can have a great time creating the splats—just know when to stop!

new york holiday cakes in black and white

I was asked to create a suite of cakes for Barneys New York, and I was only told that the store's holiday campaign would be black-and-white-themed, so I was free to run with the concept. My goal was to create a collection of ultramodern cakes that reflected the sensibility of the store's clientele and New York City's disparate visual inspirations.

NEW YORK CITY SKYLINE CAKE // This cake is
my tribute to New York and the holidays—urban with lots of bling!

BUBBLES AND GLITTER CAKE // A classic Fashion
Chef look for a sophisticated party or New Year's Eve celebration.

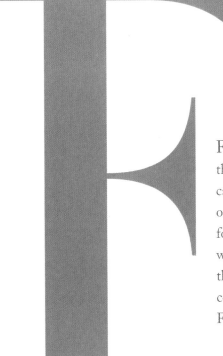

FOUR SEASONS WEDDING CAKE // I was thrilled to finally have the opportunity to design wedding cakes for same-sex couples in New York. On this particular occasion, the excitement over the pending nuptials was two-fold. First and foremost, the cake was for gentlemen clients whom I loved from the start: one always nattily dressed, the other usually stylishly scruffy—in my mind, the perfect complementary couple! Second, their event was held at the Four Seasons Restaurant.

Built on the philosophy that less is more, the Four Seasons was designed by Philip Johnson and Mies van der Rohe, two of history's most celebrated architects. Every element of the restaurant's design—from the chairs and shimmering chain curtains to the glassware—was created to celebrate the International Style. The clients' wedding was to be a large affair held in the restaurant's famous Pool Room, transformed by a giant disco ball suspended from the ceiling and dozens of candles lining the perimeter of its square pool. I wanted to find a way to link the architectural beauty, design elements, and atmosphere of the room to the cake design, which had to be both masculine and fun.

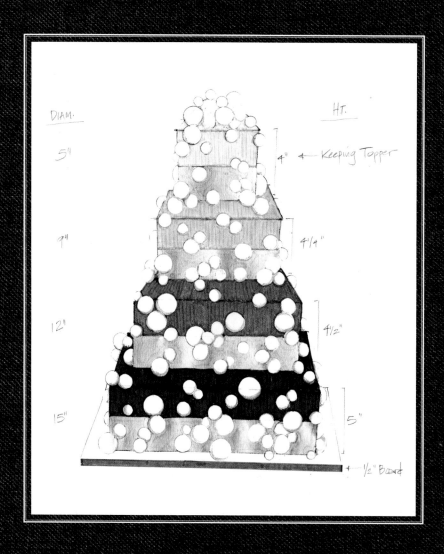

The final design featured a series of square cake tiers, inspired by ombré tones of gray flannel, each anchored by a prominent metallic silver band. Because the square pool was going to be outlined with lit candles, I chose to shower the cake with dozens of pearlized bubbles and glitter balls as a finishing touch. These decorations represented water bubbles from the fountain and points of light from the many candles and giant disco ball, thus incorporating the architecture and ambience of the space into the cake design.

Galettes Sablées (Sugar Cookies)

Makes 2 dozen cookies

A true French sugar cookie uses essentially the same recipe as tart dough, although there are many variations, as described here. I used this recipe for the round "Splat!" Cookies featured in this chapter, and I use it for all sorts of other cookie designs. I have collected cookie cutters for as long as I can remember and love using them whenever I get the chance.

INGREDIENTS

256 grams (2 cups) all-purpose flour

¼ teaspoon kosher salt

½ teaspoon baking powder

1 large egg

115 grams (1 stick) unsalted butter

200 grams (1 cup) granulated sugar

2 tablespoons whole milk

½ teaspoon pure vanilla extract

Preheat the oven to 350° F. Line 2 baking sheets or rectangular baking pans with parchment paper, and set aside.

In a medium stainless-steel mixing bowl, whisk together the flour, salt, and baking powder. In a small stainless-steel bowl, lightly beat the egg. Set both bowls aside.

In the bowl of a standing electric mixer fitted with the paddle attachment, cream the butter and sugar at high speed until well combined and fluffy. Lower the speed to medium, and slowly add the egg, milk, and vanilla. Mix well.

Finally, with the mixer on low speed, gradually add the flour mixture until just blended, being careful not to overmix.

Transfer the dough onto a work surface and shape it into 2 disks. Cover each disk securely with plastic wrap and refrigerate for a minimum of 1 hour.

When you are ready to make the cookies, roll out the dough until it is ⅛ inch thick. Using cookie cutters, cut out the cookies and place on the baking sheets. Leave at least 1 inch between each shape, as the cookies will spread when they are baked. If the kitchen is warm, the cut cookie forms may start to lose their shape. In that case, you may want to work in smaller batches of dough or refrigerate the already-cut cookie shapes before baking them.

Bake for approximately 10 minutes, or until lightly golden. Using a metal spatula, carefully place them on wire racks to cool. You may choose to decorate them with sanding sugar or Royal Icing (recipe below).

Royal Icing

Makes 3 cups

INGREDIENTS

512 grams (4 cups or approximately 1 pound) confectioners' sugar

3 tablespoons meringue powder

5 tablespoons warm water*

Gel-paste food coloring (optional)

After you measure out the sugar, sift it to remove any lumps if necessary.

In the bowl of a standing electric mixer fitted with the whip attachment, combine all the ingredients and beat until the icing forms peaks. This should take 7 minutes on low speed.

Add the gel paste food coloring, if desired. Add the color—in droplets, as the color is very concentrated—until the desired color is achieved.

If not using right away, store in the refrigerator in an airtight container for up to 3 days.

NOTE: Depending on your end use, you may desire a stiffer consistency to your icing. In that case, use 1 tablespoon less water. If you desire a thinned royal icing to decorate your cookies, add a ½ teaspoon at a time to reach your desired consistency. Remember to always use utensils that are grease-free when making royal icing.

Pearlized Gelatin Bubble Tutorial

Makes approximately 12 bubbles

Full disclosure: gelatin bubbles are time-consuming to make! You should allow 4 to 5 hours to make them and 12 to 24 hours for them to fully dry.

When making the bubbles, it's a good idea to blow up 20 to 30 percent more balloons than you think you'll need for the finished gelatin bubbles for your cake. You need to allow for wastage, because it is very difficult to control the finished surface when you are making them, and not all of them will be pretty enough to use. The finished bubbles will also vary in size, with most of them in the 1½- to 1¾-inch range.

The great news is that gelatin bubbles can be made well in advance and stored for weeks, allowing a head start on decorations for a big cake project. We keep ours in clear, airtight storage bins according to bubble diameter. The bubbles are edible, although they do not taste particularly good, so I recommend them as decoration only.

MATERIALS

15 water bomb latex balloons, 2¾-inch size

Masking tape

Wire rack

Crisco all-vegetable shortening

24 grams or 3 level tablespoons Knox unflavored gelatin

Small microwave-safe bowl

12 grams or 2 tablespoons CK Royal Pearl Super Pearl luster dust

235 milliliters (1 cup) ice cold water

Piping gel

1. Cut a 5-inch strip of masking tape for each balloon.

2. Blow up one of the balloons to 2 inches in diameter and knot it securely.

3. Create a "stem" on the balloon by stretching the balloon neck and wrapping it tightly with the masking tape, starting at the neck and working down. Continue this procedure with the remaining balloons.

4. Place the balloons, stem down, on the wire rack to hold them in place.

5. Coat the palm of your hand with a small amount of shortening.

6. Then roll each balloon in your palm to coat them with a thin layer of shortening. Wipe off any excess; otherwise, the gelatin will not stick.

7. Now make the gelatin mixture: Add 12 tablespoons cold water to 6 level tablespoons gelatin in a microwave-safe bowl. Stir gently to avoid adding air bubbles to the mixture. Microwave in 9- to 10-second intervals until the gelatin has completely dissolved.

8. Remove the bowl from the microwave and skim off any foam or undissolved gelatin. Let cool to lukewarm.

9. Add 2 tablespoons of the luster dust to the gelatin mixture and stir gently to dissolve.

10. Hold the first balloon by the stem and dip it into the mixture to coat the entire surface evenly. Let rest for a minute or so, until the mixture has set on the balloon. Repeat the dipping process, for 3 to 4 coats in total. Stir the gelatin mixture occasionally through the coating process, as the luster dust will settle to the bottom. If the mixture cools too much, place it in the microwave and set on Reheat for 4 or 5 seconds. Since the gelatin will shrink as it dries, make certain the shell is thick enough that it doesn't collapse when the balloon is popped after drying.

11. Place the balloon on the wire rack to dry. It will take the balloons approximately 12 to 24 hours to air-dry. Placing a fan on low in front of the wire rack will speed the drying time to several hours or overnight.

12. Once the balloon is dry, cut off the stem. Using your finger, gently press the balloon to help separate it from the gelatin bubble at the opening. Use a sewing needle or straight pin to puncture the balloon. Remove the balloon and use scissors to cut away the rough edges at the bubble opening.

13. When you decorate the finished cake with gelatin bubbles, the trimmed edge of the bubble will be the base that you will attach to the finished cake. Apply piping gel to the edge of the trimmed opening to secure the bubble to the cake.

IV.

THE ALLURE OF METAL

SHINY METALS CONJURE UP IMAGES OF ANCIENT AND IMAGINARY WORLDS. The development of civilization unequivocally relied on metals, and they unfailingly inspire me, whether I dream of them as prehistoric or twenty-first-century. Gleaming metallic accessories add sparkle to a fashion look, truly completing it, and the same magic applies to cake design.

There's a lot to love about metal. There is an infinite variety of metal textures—be they smooth or hammered, filigreed, or rough and pebbled. I have a huge soft spot for gold in particular and especially love using it on my cakes, whether as a monochromatic concept or as an unexpected counterpoint to brilliant color. I'm drawn to metallic tones, too, particularly lustrous metallics. Of course, there is always edible glitter, which I love to use almost as much!

I like to challenge myself to find exciting ways of combining metallic elements. Sometimes the idea can be as simple as using solid gold and iridescent gold together, as in the Iridescent Snakeskin Studded Cake (page 138). Translating the metal stud, a punk fashion–inspired accessory staple, to cake design is completely fresh territory and a perfect example of how I like to combine my love of fashion with my passion for the pastry arts. The gold studs stand out on the cake, imparting a punk-meets-couture quality. In fact, I like to think of the stud as a new form of polka dot for the chic punk set!

At the other end of the spectrum is the Valentino Filigree Cake (page 128). Here wrought-iron gates and cathedral tracery windows inspired a couture evening gown, which in turn inspired a cake that looks as if it is encased in an antique gilded cage. Metal informs fashion informs food.

Metallic surfaces are one of my favorite ways to achieve a touch of glamour and sophistication in our cakes, and those featured in this chapter illustrate a variety of methods which can be applied to great effect.

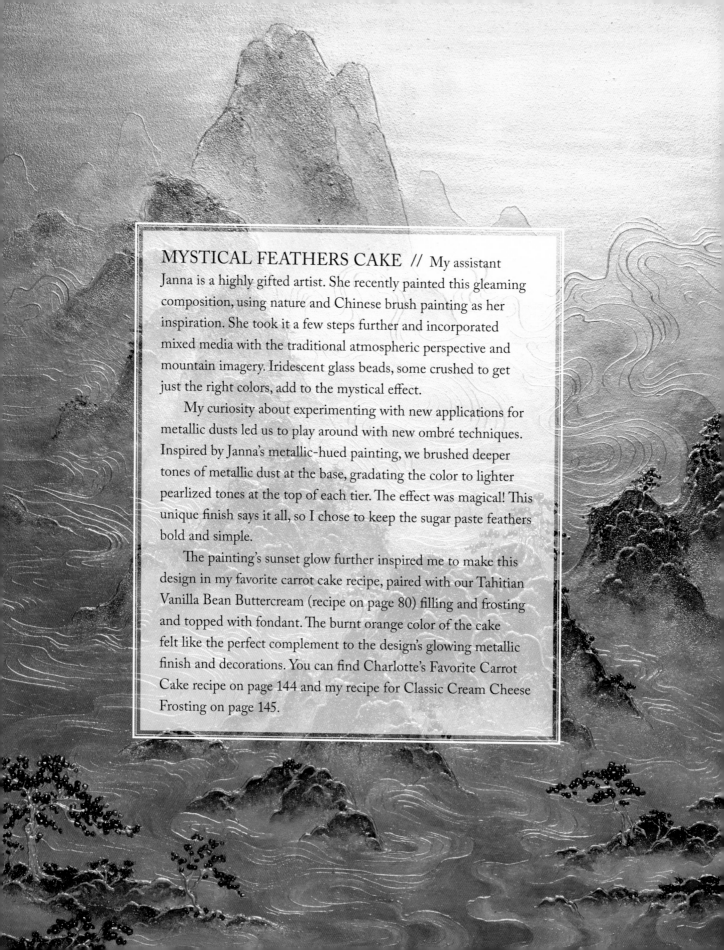

MYSTICAL FEATHERS CAKE // My assistant

Janna is a highly gifted artist. She recently painted this gleaming composition, using nature and Chinese brush painting as her inspiration. She took it a few steps further and incorporated mixed media with the traditional atmospheric perspective and mountain imagery. Iridescent glass beads, some crushed to get just the right colors, add to the mystical effect.

My curiosity about experimenting with new applications for metallic dusts led us to play around with new ombré techniques. Inspired by Janna's metallic-hued painting, we brushed deeper tones of metallic dust at the base, gradating the color to lighter pearlized tones at the top of each tier. The effect was magical! This unique finish says it all, so I chose to keep the sugar paste feathers bold and simple.

The painting's sunset glow further inspired me to make this design in my favorite carrot cake recipe, paired with our Tahitian Vanilla Bean Buttercream (recipe on page 80) filling and frosting and topped with fondant. The burnt orange color of the cake felt like the perfect complement to the design's glowing metallic finish and decorations. You can find Charlotte's Favorite Carrot Cake recipe on page 144 and my recipe for Classic Cream Cheese Frosting on page 145.

GILDED TOLE FLOWER CAKE //

The Gilded Tole Flower Cake completely fools the eye and is definitely a charter member of The Fashion Chef's "I can't believe that's a cake!" club. The cake is crafted to replicate fancy tole hand-painted metalwork, while in fact the "flowerpot" is made of our Luxe French Chocolate Cake (recipe on page 50), complete with our signature chocolate "dirt."

The stylized, sculpted lilies and leaves are a work of art unto themselves, thanks to the incredible talents of one of our team members, Ming. Ming and I have known each other since we both interned for cake maker extraordinaire Ron Ben-Israel. Ming has a fondness for detail that I admire and appreciate. He's also a math whiz, which is particularly helpful when we need to scale up our recipes to accommodate our large parties.

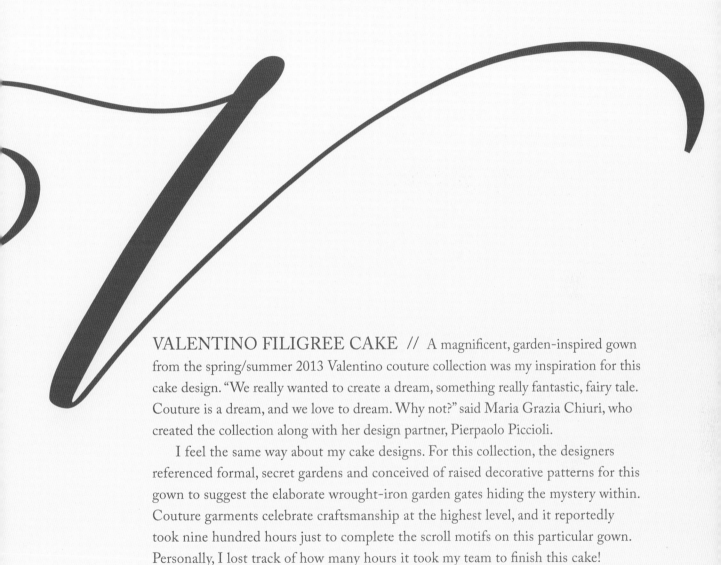

VALENTINO FILIGREE CAKE // A magnificent, garden-inspired gown from the spring/summer 2013 Valentino couture collection was my inspiration for this cake design. "We really wanted to create a dream, something really fantastic, fairy tale. Couture is a dream, and we love to dream. Why not?" said Maria Grazia Chiuri, who created the collection along with her design partner, Pierpaolo Piccioli.

I feel the same way about my cake designs. For this collection, the designers referenced formal, secret gardens and conceived of raised decorative patterns for this gown to suggest the elaborate wrought-iron garden gates hiding the mystery within. Couture garments celebrate craftsmanship at the highest level, and it reportedly took nine hundred hours just to complete the scroll motifs on this particular gown. Personally, I lost track of how many hours it took my team to finish this cake!

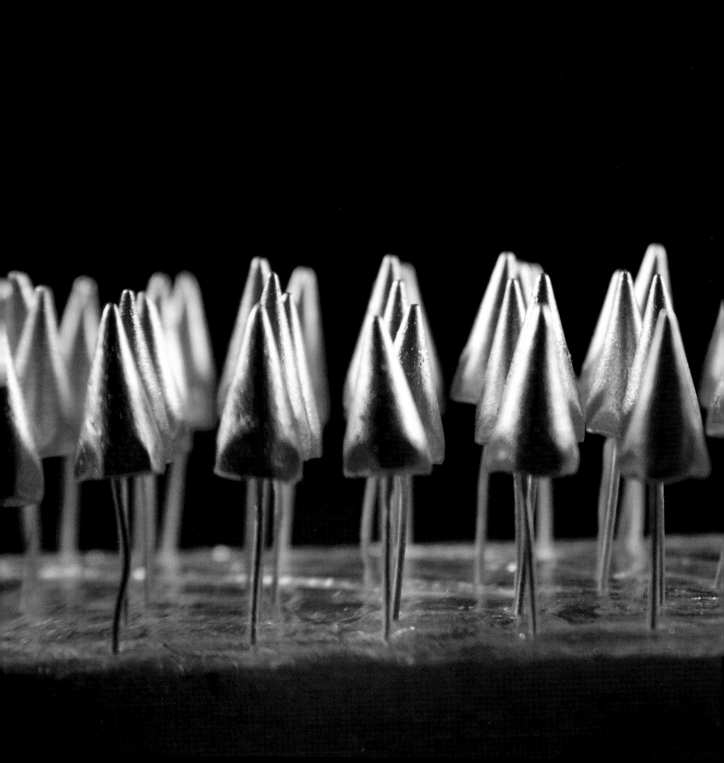

studded cakes

Metal studs are a perennial embellishment in fashion, and I became intrigued by the idea of re-creating trendy, punk-inspired studs as cake decorations, especially after realizing that I had never seen it done before. I sourced the stud shapes from trimming shops in New York's Fashion District. The team created food-safe silicone molds of each so we could test a few out. I love the idea of a spiky cake.

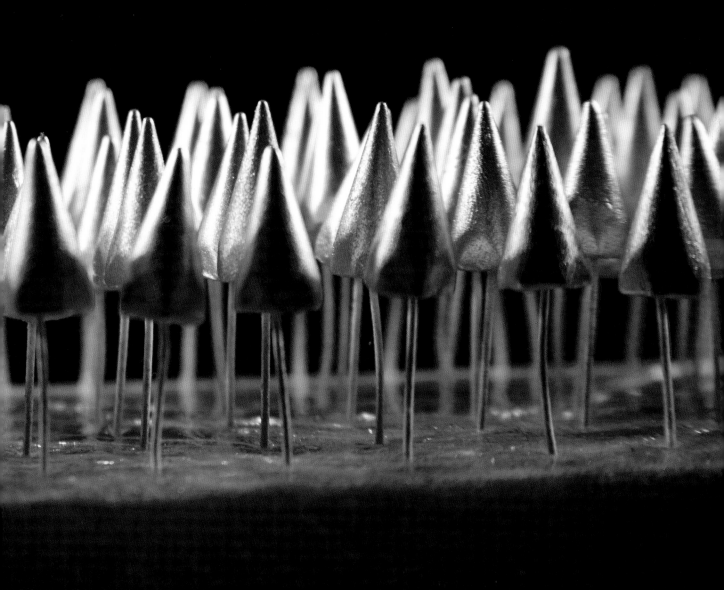

IRIDESCENT SNAKESKIN STUDDED CAKE //

One of my all-time favorite birthday cakes, this confection was created for a world-famous fashion designer.

It was an incredible honor and gift to have total creative freedom on this cake. I was able to combine my love of metallic gold and the texture of snakeskin with the studs—not to mention a sugar paste serpent watching the whole scene.

BIG FIFTY CAKE // Founded in 1964, the American Institute for Foreign Study (AIFS) is one of the oldest, largest, and most respected cultural exchange organizations in the world. With global offices in six countries, AIFS organizes cultural exchange programs for more than fifty thousand participants each year. In 2014, I had the honor of designing and creating a cake to celebrate the global organization's fiftieth anniversary at a gala held at the Waldorf-Astoria Hotel in New York City.

Fifty was a great number to highlight as the major statement for the cake, and it became my starting point for the design, along with lots of gold metallic to beautifully coordinate with the Empire Room, the ballroom where the event took place. I replaced the zero with a three-dimensional twenty-four-inch globe to symbolize the worldwide reach of AIFS. The globe's "water" was represented by a deep metallic gold, and the continents were rendered in a lighter shade of metallic to highlight the three-dimensional relief of the sugar paste construction. The finished cake was enormous, measuring in at six feet in length and just under three feet in height. The cake was a three-layer combination of my Tahitian Vanilla Bean Butter Cake (recipe on page 80) and Luxe French Chocolate Cake (recipe on page 50) and filled with my Tahitian Vanilla Bean Buttercream (recipe on page 80).

As the Big Fifty made its entrance to the party, it could be easily seen across the crowded ballroom, thanks to its metallic sheen and grand scale.

Charlotte's Favorite Carrot Cake

Serves 12

I'm a big carrot cake lover. I've tried many carrot cakes over the years, and the best carrot cake recipe I have ever come across belongs to Mollie Katzen, who published *The Moosewood Cookbook* in 1977. I loved it when I discovered it, and I still do. It is a simply delicious carrot cake. I think the key lies in the unsweetened fresh pineapple. You don't taste it much in the end, but its addition imparts texture and terrific moistness. Here is my version of that recipe.

I prefer to fill and crumb-coat this cake with my Tahitian Vanilla Bean Buttercream, followed by covering the cake in fondant. I also like the cake with a classic cream cheese frosting, so I'm including a recipe for that as well, should you prefer it. It has a fresh, lemony tang that complements the cake very nicely.

INGREDIENTS

450 grams (1 pound) carrots

225 grams (8-ounce can) unsweetened crushed pineapple, drained

400 grams (2 cups) granulated sugar

290 milliliters (1¼ cups) vegetable oil

4 large eggs

1 teaspoon pure vanilla extract

256 grams (2 cups) all-purpose flour

1½ teaspoons baking powder

½ teaspoon baking soda

2 teaspoons cinnamon

¼ teaspoon nutmeg

¼ teaspoon allspice

½ teaspoon kosher salt

115 grams (1 cup) chopped walnuts (optional)

150 grams (1 cup) raisins

Tahitian Vanilla Bean Buttercream (page 80) or Classic Cream Cheese Frosting (recipe follows)

Preheat the oven to 350° F.

Butter two 9-inch round baking pans with unsalted butter. Line the bottoms with parchment paper, then grease again and dust with flour.

Peel the carrots, then cut them into ½-inch chunks, and pulse them in the bowl of a food processor until flaked. Set aside.

In a standing electric mixer fitted with the paddle attachment, combine the sugar and oil and beat until thoroughly incorporated. Beat in the eggs, followed by the vanilla.

Sift the flour, baking powder, baking soda, cinnamon, nutmeg, allspice, and salt into a medium stainless-steel mixing bowl. Stir the dry ingredients into the egg mixture until the flour is incorporated. Do not overmix.

Fold in the flaked carrots, drained pineapple, chopped walnuts (if using), and raisins.

Pour the batter into the prepared pans and bake for approximately 30 minutes, or until a cake tester comes out clean. Remove from the oven and allow to cool on a wire rack.

Once the cakes have cooled, unmold them and fill and frost.

NOTE: Do not attempt to cover the cream cheese frosting with fondant. It will not work.

Classic Cream Cheese Frosting

This recipe yields enough to fill and frost the carrot cake.

Although we prefer to use our Tahitian Vanilla Bean Buttercream to fill and frost our carrot cakes so they can be covered in fondant, the American tradition is to use a cream cheese frosting, which I offer here as an alternative.

INGREDIENTS

115 grams (1 stick) unsalted butter

170 grams (¾ cup) cream cheese, softened

½ teaspoon lemon zest

1 tablespoon fresh lemon juice

256 grams (2 cups) confectioners' sugar

Before you begin, make sure that the sugar is not lumpy. Sift if necessary.

Cream the butter until smooth in the bowl of a standing electric mixer fitted with the paddle attachment. Add the softened cream cheese and beat until thoroughly incorporated.

Add the lemon zest and lemon juice and beat until combined.

Gradually beat in the confectioners' sugar until the frosting achieves a spreadable consistency.

V.
WHIMSY

You'll miss the best things
if you keep your eyes shut.

—Dr. Seuss, *I Can Read with My Eyes Shut*, 1978

AT THE FASHION CHEF, we try not to take ourselves too seriously—an attitude Michael and I have shared since we worked together in the fashion business. We've found that having a lighthearted approach to our work creates an environment where we are willing to take creative risks. Having a sense of humor extends to our cakes, too, and those with a touch of whimsy always make us happy.

In this chapter, the diverse interests and passions of our clients come into play in the design and execution of their cakes, which can range from incorporating a quirky element or two to a full-blown fantastical creation. In fact, one of the most enjoyable parts of what I do is to realize our clients' dreams in cake form. It's all about listening—and asking questions. At times I feel like a detective, searching for clues and taking what I discover and weaving it into a compelling and unique design that truly captures their desires.

Animals and pets are frequently a prominent component of clients' requests. We conceive these cakes as three-dimensional pet portraits and derive inspiration from an in-depth interview with the client so that I can understand the essence of the pet's personality. I prefer to do this in advance of actually seeing photographs of the subject. Successfully capturing an animal's personality in sugar paste is one of our biggest challenges and would be impossible to achieve without the great sculpting and hand-painting skills of our team.

The goal of all of the cakes in this chapter—with animals and without—is to make a personal connection come alive for our clients and their guests. These are joyous cakes, often infused with a hint of humor, sometimes unexpected, and always intended to bring about a smile.

PIG WEDDING CAKE // This client loves pigs and dreamed of them on her wedding cake.
We started by collecting miniature pig figurines, culled from our personal collections. They had to
be pigs with personality, and we ultimately settled on a family of them that the whole team liked. We
made food-safe silicone molds for each one, crafted them in sugar paste, and then carefully dusted and
hand-painted each one. We got so into the process that we freehand-sculpted others as well! Granted,
while this cake confection was quite different from those most requested—cakes featuring bouquets
of sugar paste flowers, for example—we were delighted with the results.

Not to leave her groom-to-be out of the fun, the bride surprised him with his own cake—a version

STAX ENGAGEMENT CAKE // Matt needed a little assistance from Stax, his beloved Brittany spaniel, to propose to his girlfriend, so Stax held on to the ring while Matt did the talking, and their combined effort did the trick! I'm really proud of how successfully we captured Stax's personality in hand-sculpted and hand-painted sugar paste, as we didn't have the opportunity to meet Matt's dog and had to rely on snapshot references to bring him to life.

OLIVIA CAKE // To mark the retirement of Linda van Schaick, director of Bellevue Hospital's incredible Reach Out and Read program for their bedridden children, we created a cake that represented some of her favorite books to read to the kids, *Olivia, Goodnight Moon,* and *Amos & Boris* (represented underneath Olivia's pedestal) among them. I wanted to create a three-dimensional Olivia, a figure that looked like she was coming alive, popping out from her formerly two-dimensional image on the book cover.

BLACK WATCH PLAID BIRTHDAY CAKE // Menswear designer, author, and HSN notable Jeffrey Banks has been a dear friend for many years. I jumped at the opportunity to create a special cake for a surprise birthday party given in his honor. Jeffrey has a huge collection of Scottie dog figurines (his "signature" animal), is crazy about tartans, and adores brightly colored cashmere sweaters and blankets. He is also a lover of hot dogs and all things preppy. All of this served as inspiration when I designed his cake, which incorporates sugar paste decorations tailor-made for him, down to his Stubbs & Wootton evening slippers, rendered in miniature. The party was held at Jeffrey's favorite hot dog joint in New Jersey, and the Scottie topper couldn't help but join in the feast.

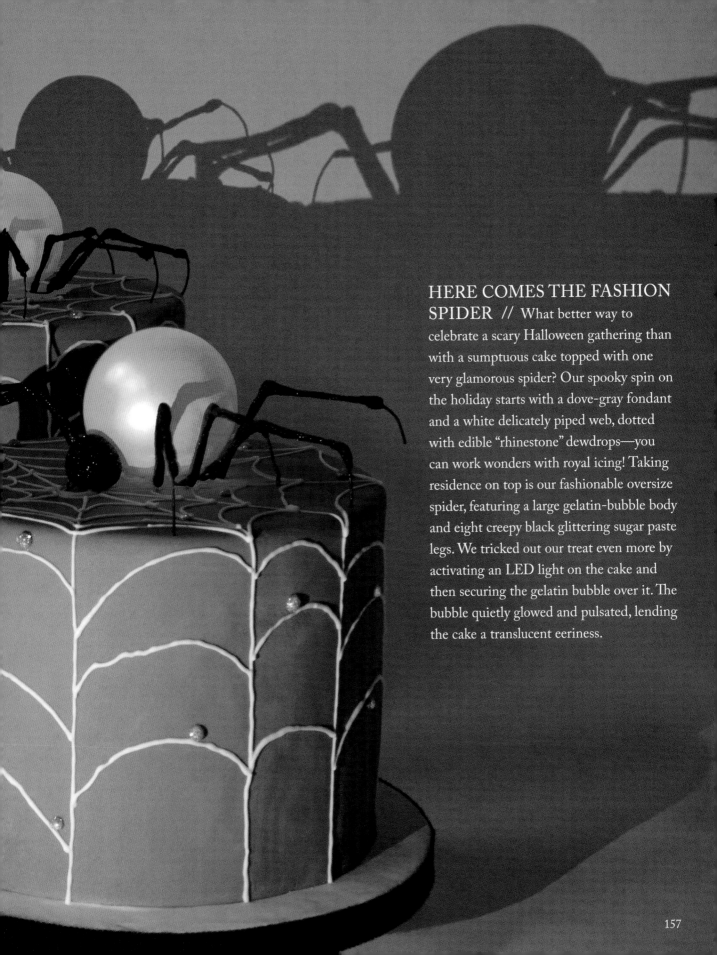

HERE COMES THE FASHION SPIDER // What better way to celebrate a scary Halloween gathering than with a sumptuous cake topped with one very glamorous spider? Our spooky spin on the holiday starts with a dove-gray fondant and a white delicately piped web, dotted with edible "rhinestone" dewdrops—you can work wonders with royal icing! Taking residence on top is our fashionable oversize spider, featuring a large gelatin-bubble body and eight creepy black glittering sugar paste legs. We tricked out our treat even more by activating an LED light on the cake and then securing the gelatin bubble over it. The bubble quietly glowed and pulsated, lending the cake a translucent eeriness.

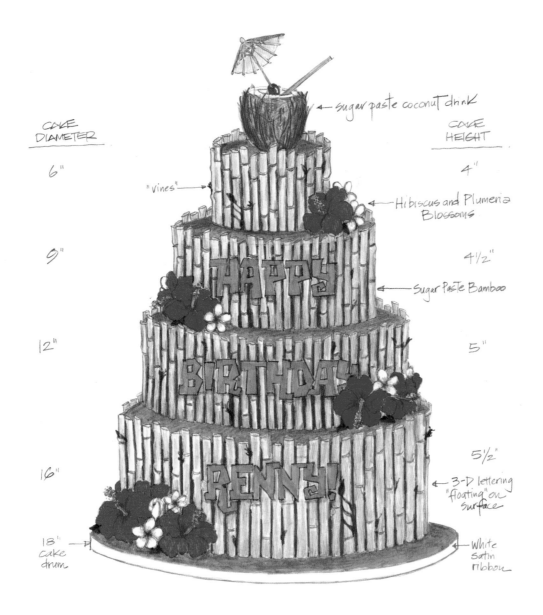

CAKE
DIAMETER

6"

9"

12"

16"

18"
cake
drum

CAKE
HEIGHT

4"

4½"

5"

5½"

← sugar paste coconut drink

"vines" →

← Hibiscus and Plumeria
Blossoms

← Sugar Paste Bamboo

← 3-D lettering
"floating" on
surface

← White
satin
ribbon

TIKI HUT BIRTHDAY CAKE // After the technical and aesthetic success of my
Woodland Fantasy Wedding Cake (page 182), I was eager to try the concept again but from a
different angle—or with a different twig, you might say! And thus the Tiki Hut Birthday Cake
was born, only this time, rather than simulating birch twigs, I was inspired to take on bamboo,
designing a blowout birthday cake with an island-vacation, tiki-hut feel. The cake was for a festive,
boisterous party with a tropical theme, and it rose to the occasion. The final design featured four
tiers of cake clad in sugar paste "bamboo." Constructed entirely of sugar paste, each length of
bamboo was made by hand and individually painted to highlight the nodes, making every piece
unique. Clusters of sugar paste hibiscus and plumeria were featured on the cake, too.

TROPICAL HIBISCUS CAKE //

The tropics, with their bright sun-drenched colors and ocean breezes, inspired this miniature hibiscus cake. Simple and refreshing, it reminds me of this summer outfit from my Charlotte Neuville sportswear collection that was featured in *Harper's Bazaar* in June 1989.

The Be Mine features The Fashion Chef's
Red Velvet Cake (recipe on page 177).
The Winged Heart cake is our exclusive
Tahitian Vanilla Bean Butter Cake paired
with our Tahitian Vanilla Bean Buttercream
(recipes on page 80).

miniature valentine cakes

These four-inch miniature cakes were inspired by vintage tattoo art, and we played around with the components of those traditional designs to come up with a modern interpretation of them. Perfectly sized for two, they are a unique way to say "I love you." In fact, they've been so popular that we now offer them in both our patisserie and our online shop in the weeks leading up to Valentine's Day.

The Kiss Me was the devilish choice, made from our Luxe French Chocolate Cake (recipe on page 50) and Tahitian Vanilla Bean Buttercream (recipe on page 80).

"THAT'S AMORE!" GROOM'S CAKE //

This groom's cake was a surprise at the couple's wedding rehearsal dinner. His fiancée asked us to create an exact replica of the pizza box used at his restaurant, down to the graphics and heart-shaped cutout vents. Needless to say, this special cake was a big hit—now that's amore!

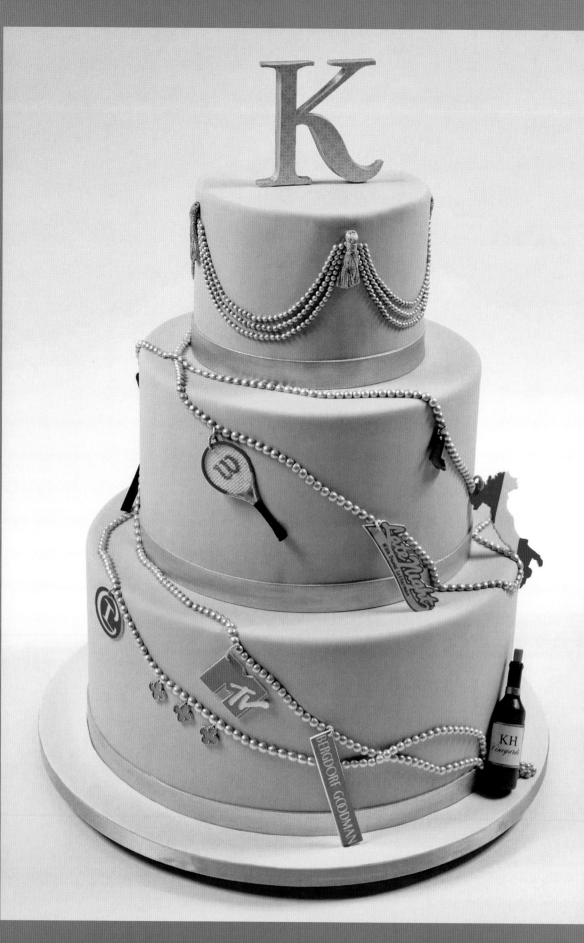

personalized cakes

Creating cakes with decorations that are customized to suit our clients' very specific fancies is a challenging, varied, and rewarding part of our work at The Fashion Chef. The following creations illustrate diverse solutions to customization that allowed us to deliver cakes that were wholly unique.

CHARM BRACELET CAKE // This cake was designed for a surprise birthday party for a client's wife. He sent us a very long inspiration list of things this dynamic woman loves. Instead of cherry-picking through his suggestions, though, I chose to combine them all together, charm bracelet–style, as I love the opportunity to personalize a cake as much as possible. We hand-made our versions of her favorite things—re-creating them as charms, including a silhouette of Italy, a Wilson tennis racket, and a Christian Louboutin stiletto heel. We further customized a miniature wine bottle by adding her initials on the label, as if she were the purveyor of her own vineyard, adding another layer of personalization to the finished cake.

CORKBOARD CAKE // Men present a special challenge when it comes to cake design, as the general mandate for most commissions is to "make it beautiful." That almost goes without saying, of course, but when the recipient is a man, I prefer to design a handsome, masculine cake. The challenge was even greater here, as the client is both a visionary entrepreneur and an authority on luxury branding and marketing. His wife presented us with an even longer list of his favorite things, which we ultimately replicated in sugar paste. Some of these references are obvious, while others are much more subtle, like the pattern on the three-dimensional M, replicated from an Hermès tie, his favorite neckwear brand. We included a sugar paste version of a sketch of the recipient that his wife provided—a quick character study rendered by a friend who would be attending the party, which provided another level of surprise. To unify all these bits and pieces, we decided to create a cake clad in faux "cork" to serve as his "inspiration" board. We then "pinned" our sugar paste versions of those items onto the cake and added sugar paste sushi, one of his favorite meals, on top. Then we went one step further and added our own bit of humor: Post-it reminders to call his wife, Louise, and to order a cake from The Fashion Chef.

VI.
INTO THE WOODS

Half the interest of the garden is the constant exercise of the imagination. You are always living three, or indeed six, months hence. I believe that people entirely devoid of imagination never can be really good gardeners. To be content with the present, and not striving about the future, is fatal.

—Mrs. C. W. Earle, *Pot-pourri from a Surrey Garden*, 1897

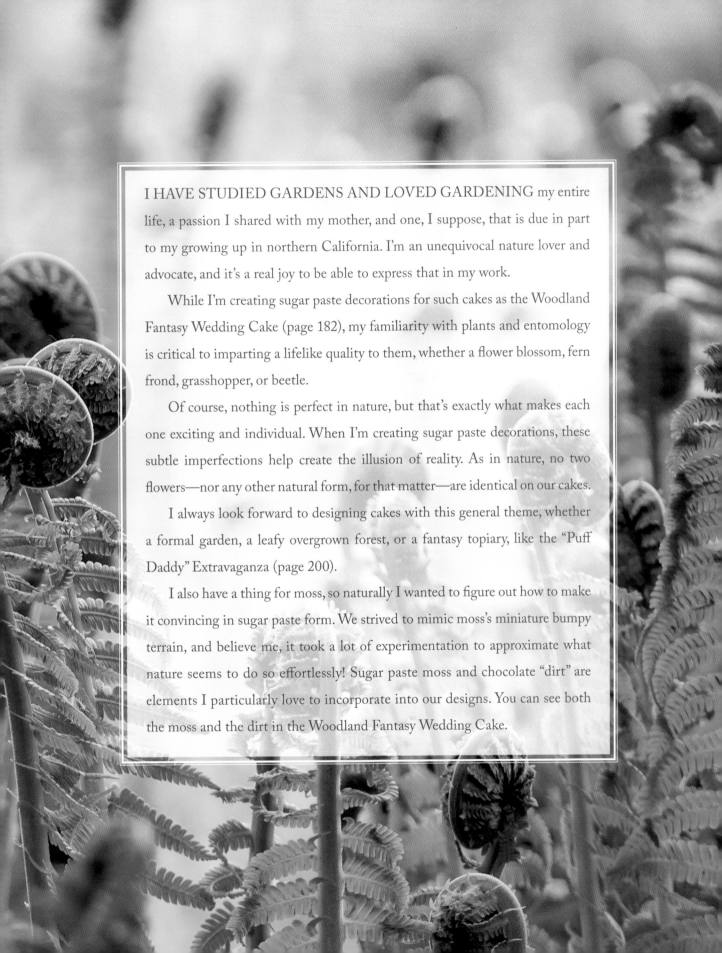

I HAVE STUDIED GARDENS AND LOVED GARDENING my entire life, a passion I shared with my mother, and one, I suppose, that is due in part to my growing up in northern California. I'm an unequivocal nature lover and advocate, and it's a real joy to be able to express that in my work.

While I'm creating sugar paste decorations for such cakes as the Woodland Fantasy Wedding Cake (page 182), my familiarity with plants and entomology is critical to imparting a lifelike quality to them, whether a flower blossom, fern frond, grasshopper, or beetle.

Of course, nothing is perfect in nature, but that's exactly what makes each one exciting and individual. When I'm creating sugar paste decorations, these subtle imperfections help create the illusion of reality. As in nature, no two flowers—nor any other natural form, for that matter—are identical on our cakes.

I always look forward to designing cakes with this general theme, whether a formal garden, a leafy overgrown forest, or a fantasy topiary, like the "Puff Daddy" Extravaganza (page 200).

I also have a thing for moss, so naturally I wanted to figure out how to make it convincing in sugar paste form. We strived to mimic moss's miniature bumpy terrain, and believe me, it took a lot of experimentation to approximate what nature seems to do so effortlessly! Sugar paste moss and chocolate "dirt" are elements I particularly love to incorporate into our designs. You can see both the moss and the dirt in the Woodland Fantasy Wedding Cake.

W

WOODLAND FANTASY WEDDING CAKE // To say every cake is special to me is not an exaggeration, but this particular one holds a very dear place in my heart.

I don't often have the opportunity to create a wedding cake for my close friends, simply because most of them are already married at this point in my life.

I made this cake for my business partner, Michael, and his now-husband, Frank, as my gift to them for their wedding day celebration. The event took place as winter turned to spring at the Bedford Post Inn, a small, chic luxury inn in Bedford, New York. Richard Gere and his then-wife, Carey Lowell, had a hand in rescuing and restoring this historic property, which dates back to the 1860s.

But back to the cake. Michael had a stack of inspiration boards for us to sort through that included many tear sheets collected from gardening and home decor magazines, pictures of all manner of flowers and ferns, and several geometric and botanical print patterns taken from textile and wallpaper references. With so many design possibilities to choose from, it was ironic that Michael, Frank, and I settled on the design direction for the cake on the spot, and one based on a single picture of a floral centerpiece. I decided to design a cake just like that, as if it were a woodland bouquet in a decorative birch twig planter. I coordinated the cake decorations closely with the tablescape decor Michael had envisioned, which included an abundance of fresh moss, woodland ferns, and crystal candlesticks. The wedding was an intimate, magical affair, and as the evening progressed a light dusting of snow began to cover the grounds.

Fern fronds are one of the most difficult forms to create in sugar paste, as they are incredibly fragile once dried. These were all handmade, along with each birch twig encompassing the cake and the ultra-delicate fritillaria blossoms—all seeming to grow from chocolate crumb "dirt." In addition to sugar paste beetles, there was a life-size, handcrafted, sugar paste grasshopper hiding on a fern for an added surpiese. The cake's every detail was crafted with the deep love I have for this incredible couple. It was so realistic, none of the guests could believe the creation was actually a cake until it was cut and served! The cake itself was our Luxe French Chocolate (recipe on page 50), with a delicious pistachio buttercream in a pale fern-green color.

MICHAEL & FRANK'S WEDDING CAKE

THE *H* // When Anna Wintour decided to host a *Great Gatsby*–themed fiftieth birthday celebration for Hamish Bowles, American *Vogue*'s European editor-at-large, at her Long Island estate, she asked me to create the dessert. I jumped at the chance!

I knew the dessert had to be something never seen before—and out of this world! Using the lush, formal gardens of *Gatsby*-era estates as inspiration, I envisioned fantasy topiary in dessert form, where guests could simply pluck off a bite-size morsel. That led to an almost three-foot-tall *H* constructed of cream puffs placed edge to edge. I submitted my sketch for approval, and once it was accepted, I frantically went about figuring out how to make the hypothetical *H* a reality!

Michael lent his talents to the design and construction of the armature, which was made of wood and sheathed in Styrofoam and finally fondant. Meanwhile, my design assistants and I worked furiously on solutions to allow the cream puffs to defy gravity. After all, hundreds of cream puffs had to somehow appear to stick to a vertical surface! Knowing a filled cream puff would be heavy for its size, we opted for a two-pronged approach: First, we inserted toothpicks into the fondant and through the Styrofoam *H* at an angle, like miniature coat hooks. Second, we used caramel as a glue, dipping each finished cream puff before attaching it to its toothpick hook.

We started with a test *H* to evaluate the proportions and to perfect the process, so the final *H* would be flawless. From this prototype we then calculated how many puffs it would take to complete the edible topiary; it came out to about 350 pieces.

Cream puffs are delicate and best consumed shortly after they are filled. We knew we had to fill and attach the puffs to the *H* on-site, right before the party, which happened to be held on my birthday. It took forever, not to mention that the *H* was dotted with miniature sugar paste fern fronds, lily leaves, and assorted petite white blossoms. I was just finishing when Anna walked in with director Baz Luhrmann, who exclaimed that profiteroles are one of Hamish's favorite desserts. That comment alone was a great birthday gift to me. And to top it off, I got home late that night with my assistant Alisa to find a group of my friends waiting to surprise me, complete with a trumpet serenade.

Altogether, it was an unforgettable evening!

A AN ARTIST AND A MUSICIAN WEDDING CAKE //

This detailed cake tells the personal story of Jane, a country-and-western singer and world-renowned artist from Texas, and Chris, a psychotherapist from Massachusetts who also likes to paint and is a rock drummer.

The cake's base tier is a replica of a snare drum. To make it as realistic as possible, we hand-sculpted the hardware and then cast it in food-safe silicone molds. It's a complex process but well worth it, as these techniques and our in-house expertise allow a measure of creativity in cake design that otherwise would not be possible.

The middle tier has a map of the United States draped on it, complete with the Lone Star State's gold emblem and a sugar paste path that travels all the way to Boston, where Jane and Chris met.

On the top tier, we hand-painted a likeness of one of Jane's beautiful screen prints. Janna, our in-house fine artist, deftly reproduced this work onto the curved surface of the fondant—a difficult task, to say the least! We re-created the tiger orchids and juniper berries in sugar paste to create the illusion of the artwork coming to three-dimensional life.

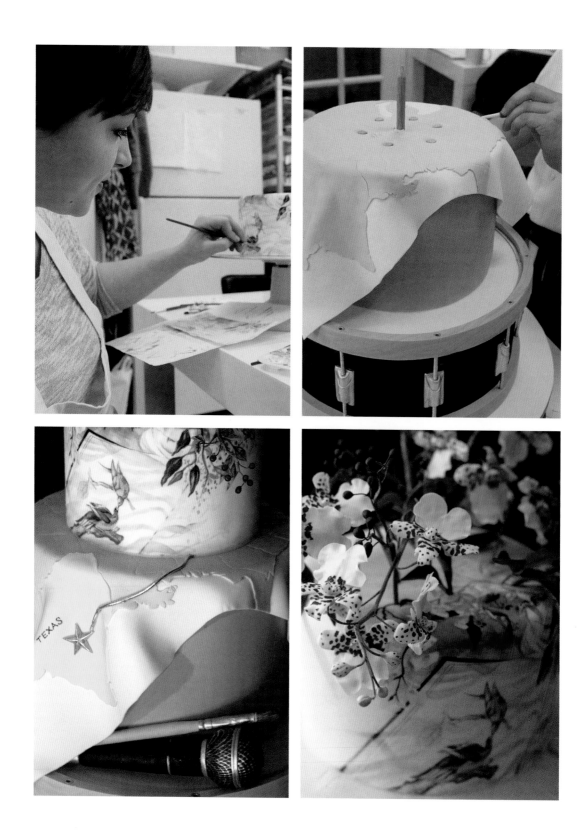

WOODLAND HOLIDAY CAKE // I designed the
Woodland Holiday Cake for the postcard The Fashion Chef includes
with every cake we deliver so that customers know how to care for
their cake upon its arrival.

The works of the seventeenth-century Dutch and Flemish
masters, especially their floral still lifes, have always inspired me,
particularly their ability to capture a vast range of blossoms in
exquisite detail. For this cake, I modified my floral assortment to
feature a wintry bouquet on a smaller scale. I strove to capture
the mood of those painted arrangements so that the finished cake
would also possess an organic, almost casual feel.

The photograph shown here is the one I selected for the postcard.
We paired it with a crimson satin ribbon for the cake box.

THE FRICK FLOWERS // Creating this extravagant sugar paste floral display for a private celebration at the Frick Collection in New York City was a unique project for me. It was the first time I created a large-scale arrangement consisting entirely of sugar paste flowers—and without cake! We collaborated with David Monn as well as Oliver Cheng Catering & Events, who created the pastillage urn for the display.

The arrangement was to be the centerpiece of an old-world-style dessert buffet. Once again, I began work by studying the seemingly inimitable floral still life paintings of seventeenth- and eighteenth-century Dutch masters. This style of painting appealed to me, as I wanted the look of my piece to feel organic and natural, like a fresh, offhandedly arranged vase of flowers. At the same time, I wanted my interpretation of these masterworks to feel as if it were an actual still life from that time, brought back to life in a new way.

The project was a real technical challenge, as the scale was huge, which meant we had to start from scratch on how to size up and then construct the flowers. Molds and cutters for many of the oversize items simply don't exist; we ultimately had to create many unique food-safe silicone molds of petals and leaves to achieve the necessary scale and floral variety. When it was time to do the final assembly, I approached it as if I were arranging live flowers—a tricky business because sugar paste flowers are very delicate. The sheer number and weight of the oversize individual flowers and leaves combined with the density of the arrangement made the assembly a very difficult and time-consuming task.

Ultimately, the twenty-eight-inch-tall arrangement consisted of 397 individual sugar paste flowers such as peonies, different varieties of garden roses, and parrot tulips. The range of foliage included fern fronds, trailing ivy branches, lily leaves, and fantastical Dusty Miller leaves. To top it off, I added unique details typical of this period of art—sprays of raspberries and a grasshopper.

FLORAL EXOTICA CAKE // This cake was inspired by my desire to create a sugar paste garden in a planter. The faux-bois planter was covered in fondant and then hand-painted to mimic natural wood. I chose an eclectic mix of cymbidium orchids, miniature country roses, fiddlehead ferns, and succulents for the bouquet. Some sugar paste moss peeks out beneath.

"PUFF DADDY" EXTRAVAGANZA // After creating the cream puff *H* for fashion editor Hamish Bowles (page 186), my design team and I were fixated on the idea of creating another cream puff dessert sculpture. As luck would have it, a month after Hamish's party, we were commissioned to create another extravagant, over-the-top dessert for an important fund-raiser in Cherry Grove, Fire Island.

Again, the theme was a *Gatsby* garden party, due largely to the popularity of Baz Luhrmann's *Great Gatsby*, his 2013 movie in wide release that summer. The garden theme inspired us to create a second "topiary." We chose a giant standard French poodle for our folly dessert—a nod to the extravagance of the party scenes in the movie, where every event was intended to raise the bar with never-before-seen spectacles.

To create the poodle, Michael made a full-scale drawing of the dog, along with drawings of faux topiaries that were intended to adorn the garden. The life-size dog armature was over three feet tall and almost four feet long. We applied the same successful toothpick-and-caramel croquembouche technique to secure the cream puffs to the dog's form. One side of the dog was clad in cream puffs that were filled with vanilla pastry cream, and the other side in chocolate-filled cream puffs. We became very fond of our subject and started calling him "Puff Daddy." The name has stuck to this day.

An incredible amount of time and talent went into sculpting the fondant and sugar paste that covered the armature. First, the wood and Styrofoam armature had to be encased in large sheets of rolled fondant, which is no easy task, given the scale. We then built up the form with sugar paste to add dimension to it and then painstakingly sculpted and painted it (with edible gel colors) to appear lifelike. This process alone took us several days. Making this dessert was truly a family affair for my team: Alisa made more than one thousand puffs, Ely deftly handled the fondant, and Janna sculpted the dog and hand-painted exquisite details on its face.

Use a pastry bag fitted with a #5 plain tip to pipe rounds of dough the size of a quarter (a little under an inch in diameter) about 3 inches apart onto the prepared baking sheets. If you desire a larger puff, increase the size of the dough round on the baking sheets and space accordingly.

Bake for 8 minutes, then reduce the oven temperature to 350° F and bake for 8 more minutes, or until the puffs are a deep golden brown. Remove from the oven and let cool to room temperature on the baking sheets, 15 to 20 minutes. Fill with pastry cream.

Pastry Cream

INGREDIENTS

32 grams (¼ cup) cornstarch

150 grams (¾ cup) granulated sugar

473 milliliters (2 cups) whole milk

4 large egg yolks at room temperature, lightly beaten

Pinch of kosher salt

2 teaspoons pure vanilla extract

2 tablespoons unsalted butter

Prepare an ice-water bath for later use in the process.

In a mixing bowl, combine the cornstarch with 50 grams of the sugar. Stir in 120 milliliters of the whole milk. Proceed by incorporating the egg yolks into the cornstarch mixture.

In a saucepan, blend the remaining 365 milliliters (1½ cups) of milk with the remaining 100 grams (½ cup) sugar and the salt. Place over medium heat and bring to a boil.

Remove the saucepan from the heat. Gradually whisk approximately one-third of the hot milk into the egg mixture. This is called "tempering" the egg yolk mixture. Whisk constantly.

Add the balance of the milk to the eggs, and return the mixture to the saucepan. Continue to cook over medium heat, constantly whisking, until the mixture comes to a boil. This procedure will take approximately 5 to 7 minutes.

When the boil is reached, beat the mixture over moderately low heat for 2 to 3 minutes to cook the cornstarch. Be careful that the custard does not scorch in the bottom of the pan.

Remove from the heat and stir in the vanilla and butter. Transfer the saucepan to the ice-water bath to halt the cooking process, and cool the pastry cream for 30 minutes.

Once the pastry cream has reached room temperature, if you are not using it right away, refrigerate it in a covered storage container and cover the surface of the cream with plastic wrap; store for up to 3 days.

VII.

JEWELED FANTASY

Then taking sharp knives they ripped the seams and pleats and let fall to the table quantities of rubies, carbuncles, sapphires, diamonds, emeralds, pearls, and other jewels of great value.

—MARCO POLO, from *The Travels of Marco Polo, the Venetian*, c. 1298

IN FASHION, particularly haute couture, luxe fabrics are often complemented by an infinite variety of embellishments— fancy feathers, ornate buttons, ribbons and braids, intricate embroidery, and, of course, jewels, faux and real.

Jewels are a constant source of inspiration for me. I've transformed our pearlized gelatin bubbles into transparent jewel-colored versions to bring ruby, emerald, sapphire, and garnet colors into cake designs, as with the Crimson Jewel Bubble Cake on page 214. The jewel bubbles further inspired me to reinvent our sugar paste glitter balls in a wild array of sparkling colors that remind me of oversize sparkling beads.

In short order, we had a whole range of rainbow colors in our glitter ball arsenal of goodies to mix and match, as seen in both the Jeweled Cakelettes (page 220) and the extra-festive Carnival Cake, a parade of color on a gold-and-white cake (page 212).

By now, dear reader, it is obvious that I love to accessorize my cakes as much as I did my fashion designs. Whether referencing fashion or not, we love to create lavish adornments for our confections. "Jeweled Fantasy" presents ravishing cake centerpieces that are memorable in style and spirit.

CARNIVAL CAKE // This cake features several of The Fashion Chef's favorite design elements. We combined a feathered topper, sugar paste glitter balls, and a mirror base to create this fantastical birthday cake. The confetti-dot background provides a visual canvas for the various adornments.

I wanted to capture the exuberance of the carnival-themed party and channel it into the cake design. Festive sugar paste masks are adorned with feathers and sprays of glass jewels. Brightly hued sugar paste glitter balls dance across the cake, and curlicues leap off the surface, mimicking party streamers blasting into the air.

CRIMSON JEWEL BUBBLE CAKE // These richly colored gelatin bubbles in tones of crimson and inky garnet create a seriously glamorous cake. Here we pair them with our dark-chocolate fondant and metallic glitter balls.

BLACK LEATHER GYPSY CAKE // This was one
of my earliest cakes, an homage to designer Joseph Altuzarra
and his fall 2012 collection. The collection was inspired by the
Italian comic book series *Corto Maltese*. Altuzarra described
its eponymous protagonist as "a sailor, his mom was a Gypsy,
and his dad was Venetian." Maltese was also a traveler and his
adventures in Morocco and India provided a premise for the
collection's Kutch Banjara–inspired dresses over-embroidered
with medallions as well as chunky knits decorated with colorful
pompons and printed with tapestry motifs. It is from this whirl
of influences that I designed the Black Leather Gypsy Cake in
honor of Altuzarra and his prodigious talent.

EMERALD SNAKESKIN CAKE // When we started experimenting with hand-painting our snakeskin-textured fondant, I fell in love, especially with creating iridescent effects. We achieve these effects by using a combination of iridescent and metallic dust colors, worked back and forth to get just the right hand-painted look. Once painted, the surface is showered with a delicate blanket of glittering gold or gently sprinkled in a variety of glitter colors, to achieve that magical iridescent quality.

The construction of the feather decorations on this design allows us to add them to a real cake, as each feather's base has been meticulously wrapped with tape and then mounted on a separate sugar paste "base" that is affixed to the cake center. As such, the feathers are not actually in contact with the cake's interior or fondant exterior. Employing this safeguard method, we occasionally use feathers to decorate real cakes. These particularly unusual black plumes add a festive note to this exotic birthday cake.

JEWELED CAKELETTES // Jeweled Cakelettes are
one of our most popular creations. Essentially four or five bites
of pure petite heaven, they are often requested as a festive party
dessert alternative. And in those cases, I draw from our whole
rainbow of glitter ball colors to coordinate with the event.

*Perched on top of the cake like a sparkling jewel, the glitter ball
is one of my favorite cake accessories.*

FELLINI CAKE // This cake was commissioned to celebrate the thirtieth wedding anniversary of one of my favorite clients, a luxury jewelry designer and his wife. As is typical of this client, who has a penchant for the outrageous and unpredictable, the venue for the celebration was a marvelous Masonic hall with elaborately painted woodwork and stained glass.

My instructions for the cake were these: "Think over-the-top love… think Fellini's *Casanova*…think Kubrick's *Eyes Wide Shut*…think…well, I trust you, Charlotte."

The inspirations and design for the cake were a mash-up of the surreal, libertine, and sometimes disturbing, elements pulled from these and other highly unusual references. I opted for a dark stained-glass color palette to complement the venue space, then spiked the colors with gold metallic to bring this cake creation to life. The resulting Fellini Cake, as it became known, features a base crafted as Fellini's giant bust of Venus emerging from the Grand Canal during the traditional Carnival in Venice, complete with her massive jeweled crown. Three tiers are hand-painted in different iridescent snakeskin colors and rich jewel tones, providing a foil for the tier that features a completely hand-painted rendering of Leonardo da Vinci's *Mona Lisa*. The antlers are a nod to the headpiece worn by Marie-Hélène de Rothschild during her famous 1972 Surrealist Ball at the Château de Ferrières. As this was an anniversary party, I thought it only fitting to top off the cake with a sinewy metallic gold snake, in reference to Adam and Eve.

The hosts and guests went wild when the cake was presented, cell-phone cameras flashing madly as a new cake celebrity made its entrance.

Our hand-painted Mona Lisa.

How to Make a Miniature Cake

Our four-inch miniature cakes are very popular for a variety of occasions. They consist of three layers of cake, typically created with Tahitian Vanilla Bean Butter Cake and Tahitian Vanilla Bean Buttercream filling (recipes on page 80).

MATERIALS

2 sheet pans

3¾-inch-diameter round pastry cutter

Sharp knife

Simple syrup

Squeeze bottle

Offset spatula

2 4-inch-diameter corrugated cardboard disks

Icing smoother or ruler

Cornstarch

250 grams (8 ounces) rolled fondant, preferably Satin Ice

Fondant roller

Fondant smoother

Palette knife

6-inch gold-foil cake board

Nontoxic glue, like Elmer's

Sugar paste, preferably Satin Ice gum paste

Clear ruler

Pizza wheel cutter

Gold metallic dust

Everclear grain alcohol

2 small bowls

Small flat-end paintbrush

Piping gel

X-Acto knife

2 small paintbrushes

1. Bake the cake in sheet pans for a finished cake thickness of 1 inch. Using the pastry cutter, press into the cake completely to cut out individual cake disks. (If you have extra disks, they can be tightly wrapped in clear plastic wrap and stored in the freezer for up to 1 month.)

2. Arrange disks on a clean sheet pan lined with parchment paper.

3. Use the knife to carefully slice off the top crust of each cake disk, and discard them.

4. Lightly and evenly moisten the surface of each cake layer with simple syrup. (For simple syrup, bring 1 cup of sugar and 1 cup of water to a boil and simmer until the sugar is completely dissolved, about 3 minutes. Remove from the heat and let cool thoroughly. The syrup can be made in advance and refrigerated in a sealed glass jar for up to 1 month.) We like to use a squeeze bottle for this purpose to better control the amount of syrup used.

8. With the offset spatula, add a generous layer of buttercream around the sides of the cake to begin the crumb-coating process.

9. Use the icing smoother to scrape away the excess buttercream to create a clean, cylindrical shape. A clean metal ruler will work for this purpose as well.

10. Dust the work surface with cornstarch, which will prevent the fondant from sticking to it. Knead and then roll out the fondant to create a round shape at least 10½ inches in diameter and approximately ⅛ inch in thickness.

11. Center the rolled fondant over the cake and gently pat the top to eliminate trapped air bubbles.

12. Using a fondant smoother, press the fondant against the cake to gently ease out the excess fondant and to eliminate fingerprints and air bubbles, creating a clean shape all around the sides.

5. Using the offset spatula, smear a small amount of buttercream on one of the corrugated cardboard disks and "glue" the first cake layer onto the disk.

6. Using the offset spatula, evenly spread ¼ inch of buttercream on top of this cake layer. Place your second cake layer directly on top and smoothly spread on another ¼-inch layer of buttercream filling. Place the third and final cake layer on top without buttercream.

7. Center the second corrugated cardboard disk on top of the third layer, being careful to line it up with the bottom cardboard disk.

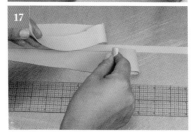

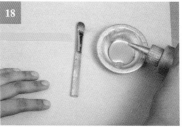

18. Combine approximately ¼ teaspoon gold dust and ¼ teaspoon Everclear alcohol (if Everclear alcohol is not available where you live, you may use vodka or lemon extract) in one of the small bowls. Mix until you achieve a consistency resembling melted ice cream.

13. Trim away the excess fondant on the bottom with a palette knife, being careful to press the knife down onto the worktable. Do not press against the sides of the cake, as it will damage the fondant.

14. Cut and peel away a 3-inch-diameter circle from the center of the gold-foil cake board. Make sure to cut away only the foil. Use a small amount of nontoxic glue on the cut-out area and center the cake on the board. The glue will ensure that the cake remains centered and attached to the board.

15. Take a small piece of the sugar paste (we mix a yellow tone) and roll out a shape large enough to cut a 14 × ½–inch band.

16. Use the clear ruler and pizza cutter to measure and cut the band.

17. Peel away the excess.

19. Paint the top and sides of the sugar paste band with the gold dust mixture, using the small flat-end paintbrush.

22. Use the X-Acto knife to neatly trim away the excess for a nice clean seam on the band. You will want this seam to be at the back of the cake.

You now have a miniature cake "canvas" to decorate as you wish!

20. To secure the gold band in place, add a small amount of piping gel to the second small bowl and apply a very thin layer of piping gel all around the base of the cake.

21. Carefully wrap the gold band around the cake base and overlap the band where the ends meet.

Acknowledgments

This book is a dream come true. So many extraordinary people have inspired me and contributed to this creation, whether they knew it or not. My deep gratitude goes to:

Michael. My closest of friends and my perfect business and creative partner. You complete me. Thank you for your listening, your patience, and, above all, your insanely wonderful take on life itself.

Elizabeth Viscott Sullivan. The best editor Michael and I could ever imagine having. Thank you for your deep experience and knowledge of your craft, and, most of all, your hilarious sense of humor. We are forever Fondantly Yours.

Lynne Yeamans. We wanted you to design our book from the very beginning. We had a thousand ideas at once and thank you for graciously indulging us with variations on layouts, fonts, and color choices at the eleventh hour and at a rapid pace. We could not have accomplished this without your incredible skills and designer's eye—and the results are that much more beautiful as a result.

Nell, my most beautiful creation. Ever. Your sense of style and beauty, your fierce intelligence, and your talent never cease to amaze me. I love you.

To our extraordinary design team, Ely, Janna, Ming, Shannie, and Juan. The Fashion Chef would not exist without your talents. You make it bigger every day.

Alisa. My first design assistant. Thank you for your inimitable talent. I will never forget the Broadway show tunes that got us through decorating those first cakes into the wee hours of the morning.

Circe Hamilton, photographer extraordinaire. We would not have these beautiful cake photographs were it not for your talent and vibrant personality—not to mention your extremely flexible shooting schedule! We love you for all these things and are very grateful.

Roy Assad. My confidant and friend. There are no words to thank you for your selflessness, your coaching, and your love.

Frank Borsas. Your support and vote of confidence have made it possible for Michael and me to join forces. We love you and are both so very grateful.

Jeffrey Banks. My "surrogate husband," escort extraordinaire, and close friend. Thank you for your coaching and unflaggingly encouragement over the years for my fashion company and now for The Fashion Chef.

Amy Natkins Lipton. You inspire me. Thank you for listening, your limitless curiosity, and your friendship. It means the world to me.

Ed Filipowski and Mark Lee. You were both there for me from the very start to lend your enthusiasm and support. I am most appreciative.

Nancy Sloan Alchek. I simply love working with you! Many thanks for your trust and early belief in The Fashion Chef.

David Monn. We were born under the same reeds. I so appreciate your steadfast support, and for sharing your boundless talent and unerring vision.

Ken. My former husband, Nell's father, and The Fashion Chef's one-and-only KDS delivery person. Thank you for making it fun.

Madeleine. My sister and my best companion throughout those early years.

My father, Jacques. No words can express my gratitude for your gifts of drawing, color, and creativity, and for surrounding us with beauty and style.

My mother, Christiane. When I lost you, I lost my best friend and my wisest counselor. You taught me what it is to be a brave human being.

Our clients. You never cease to amaze and delight. You reinvent The Fashion Chef with every new conversation. Thank you for believing in what we do and how we do it.

Bibliography

Bowles, Hamish. "Valentino/Spring 2013 Couture." Review. *Vogue,* January 23, 2013. http://www.vogue.com/fashion-week/spring-2013-couture/valentino/review/ (accessed July 2, 2014).

Dr. Seuss. *I Can Read with My Eyes Shut.* New York: Random House, 1978.

Earl, Maria Theresa. *Pot-pourri from a Surrey Garden.* London: Smith, Elder & Co., 1897.

Ephron, Nora. *Heartburn.* New York: Alfred A. Knopf, 1983.

Garten, Ina. http://www.foodnetwork.com/recipes/ina-garten/beattys-chocolate-cake-recipe.html (accessed August 6, 2014).

Jefferson, Thomas. *Thomas Jefferson Quotes.* www.jeffersonquotes.com/2012/07/walk-about-paris.html (accessed July 2, 2014).

Phelps, Nicole. "Fall 2012 Ready-to-Wear Altuzarra." Style.com, February 10, 2012. http://www.style.com/fashionshows/review/F2012RTW-ALTZRRA/ (accessed July 2, 2014).

Polo, Marco, and William Marsden. *The Travels of Marco Polo, the Venetian.* New York: Boni & Liveright, 1926.

Select Sources

Lee's Art Shop
A comprehensive selection
of art and graphic supplies.

220 West 57th Street
New York, NY 10019
(212) 247-0110
www.leesartshop.com

Utrecht Art Supplies
Quality, professional artist
materials, paintbrushes, etc.

www.utrechtart.com

BAKING SUPPLIES

Amazon
www.amazon.com

Amoretti
Pastry, savory, and beverage
flavorings and ingredients.
I am particularly fond of this
company's compounds and
artisan natural flavors.

451 Lombard Street
Oxnard, CA 93030
(805) 983-2903
www.amoretti.com

CK Products
(888) 484-2517
www.ckproducts.com

Crown Maple
Simply the best organic maple
syrup that we have found to flavor
our cakes and buttercreams.

Madava Farms
47 McCourt Road
Dover Plains, NY 12522
(845) 877-0640
www.crownmaple.com

Fancy Flours
www.fancyflours.com

JB Prince
36 East 31st Street, 11th Floor
New York, NY 10016
(212) 683-3553
www.jbprince.com

La Cuisine
My go-to resource to track down
all manner of flavoring extracts
and European flavoring essences.

www.lacuisineus.com

L'Epicerie
Professional-grade products, as
well as hard-to-find ingredients
made available to the home pastry
chef in manageable quantities.

(866) 350-7575
www.lepicerie.com

**New York Cake & Baking
Distributor**
"The one and only" cake and
baking emporium located in
New York City.

56 West 22nd Street
New York, NY 10010
(212) 645-2253
www.nycake.com

**The Perfect Purée of
Napa Valley**
Fruit purees and concentrates,
with wonderful customer
service to boot!

2700 Napa Valley Corporate Way,
   Suite L
Napa, CA 94558
(800) 556-3707
www.perfectpuree.com

Pfeil & Holing
A supplier of all manner of
cake-decorating materials, with
excellent customer service.

5815 Northern Boulevard
Flushing, NY 11377
(718) 545-4600
www.cakedeco.com

Satin Ice Fine Foods, Inc.
My resource for the best commercially made rolled fondant and gum paste / sugar paste. If you do not have a local distributor, you can order it directly from CK Products (see listing on page 236).

Satin Ice Rolled Fondant
     and Gum Paste
32 Leone Lane, Unit 1
Chester, NY 10918
(845) 469-1034
www.satinice.com

Thermapen
The best instant-read thermometer out there. A must-have!

www.thermoworks.com

LED LIGHTS

Fortune Products, Inc.
Our resource for all manner of LED products.

2824-A Old Hartford Road
Lake Stevens, WA 98258
(425) 334-9739
www.fortuneproducts.com

MOLDS AND CUTTERS

Etsy
www.etsy.com

First Impressions
One of the best resources for food-safe silicone molds.

300 Business Park Way,
     Suite A-200
Royal Palm Beach, FL 33411
(561) 784-7186
www.firstimpressionsmolds.com

Geraldine's Creative Cutters
561 Edward, L4C 9W6
Ontario, Canada
(905) 883-5638
store.creativecutters.com

Global Sugar Art
One of the best resources for cake-decorating supplies, food-safe silicone molds, cutters, boxes, boards, etc.

(800) 420-6088
www.globalsugarart.com

PRESENTATION SUPPLIES

BRP Boxes
Cake boxes.

1905 Lincoln Way
Clinton, IA 52732
(563) 243-5210
www.brpboxshop.com

Dallas Foam
White laminate cake drums.

5901 Park Vista Circle
Keller, TX 76248
(800) 275-6177
www.dallas-foam.com

RIBBONS, FEATHERS, AND EMBELLISHMENTS

B&Q Trim Store
102 West 38th Street
New York, NY 10018
(212) 869-6889
www.shinetrim.com

Dersh Feather & Trading Corporation
144 West 37th Street, Suite 4B
New York, NY 10018
(212) 714-2806
www.dershfeather.com

M&J Trimming
1008 Avenue of the Americas
New York, NY 10018
(800) 965-8746
www.mjtrim.com

Shine Trims
A smaller outpost of B&Q Trim (see listing above).

210 West 38th Street
New York, NY 10018
(212) 869-8887
www.shinetrim.com

U.S. Box
Grosgrain and satin ribbons.

www.usbox.com

American and Metric Conversions

AMERICAN VOLUME MEASUREMENTS

1 Tablespoon				= ½ Fluid Ounce	= 3 Teaspoons
1 Cup				= 8 Fluid Ounces	
1 Pint			= 2 Cups	= 16 Fluid Ounces	
1 Quart		= 2 Pints	= 4 Cups	= 32 Fluid Ounces	
1 Gallon	= 4 Quarts	= 8 Pints	= 16 Cups	= 128 Fluid Ounces	

AMERICAN VOLUME TO METRIC VOLUME (LIQUID)

1 Fluid Ounce			= 29.57 Milliliters
1 Teaspoon			= 5 Milliliters
1 Tablespoon	3 Teaspoons		= 15 Milliliters
1 Cup	½ Pint		= 236.6 Milliliters
1 Pint	2 Cups	= 0.473 Liter	= 473 Milliliters
1 Quart	2 Pints	= 0.946 Liter	= 946 Milliliters
1 Gallon	4 Quarts	= 3.78 Liters	

Formula: # Fluid Ounces x 29.57 = # Milliliters per # Fluid Ounces
e.g. To determine the metric equivalent of 15 Fluid Ounces: 15 x 29.57 = 443.6 Milliliters

AMERICAN WEIGHT TO METRIC WEIGHT

1 Ounce	= 28.37 Grams
1 Pound (16 Ounces)	= 454 Grams

METRIC WEIGHT TO AMERICAN WEIGHT

1 Kilogram (1000 grams)	= 2.2 Pounds	= 35.2 Ounces
1 Gram		= .035 Ounce

Formula: # Grams divided by 28.37 = # Ounces per # Grams
e.g. To determine the ounce equivalent of 500 Grams
500 divided by 28.37 = 17.62 Ounces = 1 Pound 1.62 Ounces

OVEN TEMPERATURE EQUIVALENTS

Fahrenheit	Celsius	Gas Mark	Description
225	105	¼	Cool
250	120	½	
275	135	1	Very slow
300	149	2	
325	162	3	Slow
350	176	4	Moderate
375	190	5	
400	204	6	Moderately hot
425	218	7	Fairly hot
450	232	8	Hot
475	246	9	Very hot
500	260	10	Extremely hot

TEMPERATURE CONVERSION FORMULAS

Degrees Fahrenheit to degrees Celsius:
[(F degrees minus 32) x 5] divided by 9 = degrees Celsius
  e.g. 212 Degrees F. converted to Degrees Celsius
  [(212 degrees F. minus 32) x 5] divided by 9 = 100 degrees Celsius

Degrees Celsius to degrees Fahrenheit:
[(Degrees Celsius x 9) divided by 5] + 32 = Degrees Fahrenheit
  e.g. 37 degrees Celsius converted to Degrees Fahrenheit
  [(37 degrees Celsius x 9) divided by 5] + 32 = 98.6 degrees